AGENDA

Requiem: The Great War

AGENDA

CONTENTS

ESSAYS

POEMS

ESSAYS

CHOSEN BROADSHEET POETS

NOTES FOR BROADSHEET POETS

Front cover: David Jones:
frontispiece for *In Parenthesis*
with permission of the Jones Estate/National
Museum of Wales

Introduction

'Have you forgotten yet?'...
          Siegfried Sassoon: 'Aftermath'

Let Siegfried Sassoon's haunting question introduce this commemorative special issue of *Agenda* in which honouring must, above all, be given to the War poets such as Sasoon, Owen, whose extraordinarily powerful poems, written while on the Front, serve not only as important historical documents, but as outstanding examples of poetry written in extremity, at the edge of experience: where poetry braves and dares.

Here, we not only mark the centenary of that war, without glorifying it, but testify to the fact that all of us alive now, in the relatively early twenty first century, are the last generation to have actually known, or heard first hand about, those who fought in the war, often giving up their lives. The very fine poet, Michael Longley, is an example of someone whose father fought in World War 1 and, as evident in these pages, he writes powerfully on this theme, explaining how his poems glance off World War 1 with different angles and perspectives.

With essays on French, German, Italian and Russian poetry of the Great War, it is hoped that a universal overview is given of poetic output, and indeed of soldierly experience, and that a balanced outlook is achieved.

As most readers and subscribers might know, or not know, the *Agenda* logo letterhead was created especially for *Agenda* by the hand of David Jones, himself an artist and poet of the Great War. How this came about was always up till now unclear. But thanks to Thomas Dilworth, the close relationship between *Agenda*, William Cookson (*Agenda*'s founding editor, along with Pound), and David Jones, is clarified here.

The poets in these pages have been chosen for responding in their own unique way to the Great War, each of them perhaps being, as Virginia Woolf suggested, 'a poet in whom live all the poets of the past, from whom all poets in time to come will spring', linking them to the great Chain of Being. Indeed, as James Aitchison suggests, in his useful and inspiring book, *New Guide to Poetry and Poetics* (Rodopi, Amsterdan, New York 2013), 'all poems are part of a great universal poem, a living force that is continually revitalized and extended by new poems'. He quotes Auden also as defining 'a vision of a kind of literary All Souls Night in which the dead,, the living and the unborn writers of every age and in every tongue were seen as engaged upon a common, noble and civilising task'. With this idea in mind, then, of poets being bound together, let all voices chime in urgently with Siegfried Sassoon's beginning and end refrains in 'Aftermath':

Have you forgotten yet?...
Look down, and swear by the slain of the War that you'll
    never forget...

Have you forgotten yet?...
Look up, and swear by the green of the Spring that you'll
    never forget.

Patricia McCarthy

Tom Dilworth

William Cookson, David Jones, and *Agenda*

David Jones and William Cookson were friends before the founding of *Agenda*. In 1955, a Westminster schoolmate of Cookson, Edmund Gray (son of Nicolete Gray, a friend of Jones since 1929) introduced them. Cookson was sixteen, Jones sixty. Together the schoolboys visited him in his room in Northwick Lodge in Harrow. He was poor, and they chipped in to buy him a little Russian radio.[1] Cookson was soon visiting about once a month. He liked how Jones spoke to him as an equal and how his smile lit up his face.[2] Cookson was sensitive, gentle, and appreciative. Open to modernism, his chief literary enthusiasm was Ezra Pound. Jones told Cookson about reading some of the Cantos, including the Pisan Cantos, in 1952. Seeing the similarity with his own work and fearing influence, he had decided to read no more. But he loved the Usury Canto and the bit on the war in 'Mauberley.' He and Cookson spoke about the whole of English literature, Jones telling him that he liked poetry in Scotts, especially the work of a poet Tom Scott (1918-95). He also said he liked Michael Alexander's translation of 'The Battle of Maldon.' But instead of reading modern poets, he reread his favourites, though he felt slightly guilty about this. When Cookson visited Pound for a week in 1958 and told him about Jones and his epic-length poems, Pound complained, 'The Possum never let me know about him.'[3]

In January 1959, with Pound's encouragement, Cookson founded the little magazine *Agenda,* purely because he loved poetry – he was teaching English to earn a living and devoted his weekends to editing the magazine. Jones regarded this as 'heroic', thought *Agenda* 'well worth supporting', and offered to help.[4] Cookson asked him to provide lettering for the title and contents page. On 28 July 1961, Jones sent two inscriptions, the words 'AGENDA' and 'CONTENTS', in time to appear in volume 2, number 5. They have appeared in every issue since. Jones sought (and received) no payment for this or anything else he contributed to *Agenda*.

The magazine and Cookson were important encouragements to him as a poet. Cookson asked him for something to publish, and since Jones thought the magazine 'should be encouraged', in 1961 he set to work on 'The Hunt', a poem about Arthur (as embodiment of pagan gods and Christ) and his

[1] William Cookson, letter to author 12 February 1990
[2] W. Cookson, letter to author 14 June 1988.
[3] W. Cookson interviewed by author 14 June 1988.
[4] David Jones, letter to Tony Stoneburner 30 August 1963. For permission to publish from Jones's letters I am grateful to the trustees of David Jones's estate.

followers chasing the land-wasting Twrch Trwyth (Great Boar), from the story of 'Culhwch and Olwen' in *The Mabinogion*. He was slow to finish it, so in 1963 he let Cookson have 'The Tutelar of the Place', which had been published in *Poetry* in 1961. In 1965 he gave Cookson 'The Hunt', modestly asking whether it would be all right.[5] Then he brought out an old Ordnance Survey map, laid it on the bed, and indicated to him the track taken by the boar Trwyth.[6] He made changes in the text down to the deadline for submission. 'The Hunt' is one of the best lyric poems of the century, the most accessible of Jones's important poems, and, in my view, the first one by Jones that anyone should read. But it is not anthologized and is therefore virtually unknown. It and 'The Tutelar' are his most lyrically musical poems.

Cookson decided in the autumn of 1966 to combine three issues of *Agenda* into a special issue on Jones, who contributed all but one five mid-length poems that he had completed in the past fourteen years— the exception being 'The Tribune's Visitation', which was reserved for separate book publication. Moved by Cookson's decision, Jones began a poem entitled 'The Sleeping Lord' also for inclusion if he could finish it on time for submission in February 1967.[7] It concerns the despoliation of the Welsh landscape, cultural loss, and Christianty as hope for cultural revival. For five months, he worked on it exclusively, 'to the neglect of all else' including accumulating correspondence, working sometimes till four in the morning.[8] Finished in time, at twenty-seven pages, it is probably the single great ecological literary work of the twentieth century. It would be his last complete, substantially new poem. That he could write something so impressive at this late date is cause to be grateful to Cookson and *Agenda* for providing an incentive for him to write it.

In late June 1967, the special issue appeared, the first book-length publication devoted to Jones's work.[9] It 'turned out *far* better' than Jones 'had dared to hope', and knowing how hard Cookson had worked with printers, Jones told him how grateful he was and congratulated him on the quality especially of the reproductions, some of which had to be redone four times.[10] Of the contributions to the issue by others, he thought the best were essays by Nancy Sanders and Stuart Piggott. Both, he thought, approached his work with rare objectivity and perception.[11] Of these he

---

[5] W. Cookson interviewed by author,14 June 1988
[6] W. Cookson interviewed by author,14 June 1988
[7] D. Jones, letter to W. Cookson, 20 March 1967.
[8] D. Jones, letter to ·to T. Stoneburner, Sat-Sun February 1967.
[9] ·D. Jones, letter to T. Stoneburner, 15 May 1967.
[10] D. Jones, letter to T. Stoneburner, 25 June 1967.
[11·] D. Jones, letter to Bernard Wall, 1 July 1967.

thought Piggott's essay 'the best in many ways,' 'a relief from all this blasted "art" & "literary" criticism', and he admired (and envied) its 'very clear concise English'.[12]

The special issue was a turning point for *Agenda*. Previously, it was not much noticed by the press, and Jones had regretted this for Cookson's sake.[13] Now it was mentioned and reviewed by the *Irish Times* and the *Guardian*. One sentence in the latter greatly amused Jones: 'This present number, running to 176 pages, is so attractively designed that sixth-form schoolgirls will want to eat it.'[14] It was also reviewed in the *Spectator*, the *TLS*, and the *Tablet*. These reviews brought the magazine to national attention. The issue soon sold out, so that in November Cookson had another thousand copies printed. This success enabled him to get a substantial Arts Council grant to help with publication and, thereafter, to obtain more generous subsidies.[15]

The special issue also brought Jones new prominence. For many, who considered him chiefly a visual artist, the five substantial mid-length poems in the special issue were revelatory. Among his friends impressed by these were Hugh and Antonia Fraser, who concluded that their appreciation of him had been incomplete, that he was a poet of great importance.[16] Jones's new notoriety resulted in his winning the first City of London Midsummer Prize in 1968, for a Londoner practising one or more of the arts who had made 'an outstanding contribution to Britain's culture'. It may also lie behind his being made a Companion of Honour in 1974.

He wanted to put together a new book of poetry and discussed this with Cookson. Visiting on 20 July1971, Cookson suggested that the volume consist solely of the already published poems. Jones liked this idea. Cookson assembled the poems for delivery to Faber.[17] In October 1973 he and Jones each corrected a set of galleys, and in mid-November collated corrections. *The Sleeping Lord and other fragments* was published on 25 March 1974.[18] More than any other collection or sequence in English, they test traditional values in the face of technological pragmatism, political totalitarianism, and modern mechanised war. The best review 'by far' of this book was, Jones thought, by Seamus Heaney in *The Spectator*, who praised Jones as 'an extraordinary writer' who has 'returned to the origin and brought something

---

[12.] D. Jones, letter to René Hague, 19 June 1967.

[13] D. Jones, letter to B. Wall, 17 July 67

[14.] D. Jones, letter to R. Hague 15 August 1967.

[15.] D. Jones in conversation with T. Stoneburner, written record, 26 May 1969; D. Jones, letter to Herbert Read, unposted, 18 Nov 1967.

[16.] Antonia Fraser-Pinter interviewed by author, 5 August 1987.

[17] W. Cookson, letter to D. Jones 29 October 1972,.

[18] D.Jones, letter to W. Cookson 24 March 1974;D. Jones to R. Hague 26 February 1974.

back, something to enrich not only the language but people's consciousness of who they have been and who they consequently are'. Decades later W.S. Merwin would call these poems 'some of his great splendours'.[19]

Before helping him with *The Sleeping Lord*, Cookson had done Jones an important service. In the decades since their first publication, Jones's long poems, *In Parenthesis* (1937) and *The Anathemata* (1952), had not been included in Faber's list of poetry. Nor had Jones been listed on dust jackets among the poets Faber published. This mistake helps to explain the decades-long failure of academic critics to assess Jones's long poems as poetry. In the spring of 1970, Cookson wrote a letter of protest to Peter du Sautoy at Faber.[20] Only with difficulty was du Sautoy able to convince Charles Monteith, the poetry editor, who thought Jones's work generically borderline because half of *In Parenthesis* is not verse, which he naively thought poetry had to be.[21] But the correction was made in the summer of 1970. About genre, Jones at least had no doubts: 'It's either poetry, of sorts, or *nothing at all.*'[22]

Note

Enthusiasts of David Jones might like to know that special copies of works by David Jones are available from Agenda Editions:

The Kensington Mass (Agenda Editions, 1975) (a work David Jones was working on at the time of his death)

Letters to William Hayward, edited by Colin Wilcockson (Agenda Editions, 1979)

The Roman Quarry and other sequences, edited by Harman Grisewood and René Hague (Agenda Editions, 1981)

The above books are available from the *Agenda* office, The Wheelwrights, Fletching Street, Mayfield, East Sussex TN20 6TL.
Email: admin@agendapoetry.co.uk

---

[19] Durrant clipping n.d.; W. Merwin, letter to author. 7 April 2008.
[20] Herbert Read, letter to Peter du Sautoy 28 October 1970.
[21] P. du Sautoy, letter to H. Read 22 July 1970; Charles Monteith to Mr Crawley 16 March 1970.
[22] D. Jones to Jackson Knight 31 July 1951.

Michael Longley

Out of the Smoke

Great War Poems 1965-2014: A Selection

My obsession with the Great War begins and ends with my father. At the age of eighteen he enlisted in the London Scottish in September 1914 at Buckingham Gate in London. A year later he took his commission with the Queen's Regiment. He saw action at the Battle of the Somme and the Battle of Loos, and was wounded at High Wood. Promoted to Captain and barely out of his teens, he commanded a Company who were nicknamed Longley's Babies: many of them shaved only occasionally and some not at all. He was awarded the Military Cross for gallantry. Miraculously, he survived the trenches for the duration of the war. I wish now that my twin brother Peter and I had asked him more questions about the nightmare. He did show us the shrapnel wound on his shin and a stain on his shoulder where he had been burned by mustard gas. However, like many survivors he preferred not to talk about his experiences. I wrote 'In Memoriam' in Spring 1965. It quotes from the wonderful songs the Tommies sang in the trenches and, at its close, echoes Wilfred Owen.

In Memoriam

My father, let no similes eclipse
Where crosses like some forest simplified
Sink roots into my mind; the slow sands
Of your history delay till through your eyes
I read you like a book. Before you died,
Re-enlisting with all the broken soldiers
You bent beneath your rucksack, near collapse,
In anecdote rehearsed and summarised
These words I write in memory. Let yours
And other heartbreaks play into my hands.

Now I see in close-up, in my mind's eye,
The cracked and splintered dead for pity's sake
Each dismal evening predecease the sun,
You, looking death and nightmare in the face

With your kilt, harmonica and gun,
Grow older in a flash, but none the wiser
(Who, following the wrong queue at The Palace,
Have joined the London Scottish by mistake),
Your nineteen years uncertain if and why
Belgium put the kibosh on the Kaiser.

Between the corpses and the soup canteens
You swooned away, watching your future spill.
But, as it was, your proper funeral urn
Had mercifully smashed to smithereens,
To shrapnel shards that sliced your testicle.
That instant I, your most unlikely son,
In No Man's Land was surely left for dead,
Blotted out from your far horizon.
As your voice now is locked inside my head,
I yet was held secure, waiting my turn.

Finally, that lousy war was over.
Stranded in France and in need of proof
You hunted down experimental lovers,
Persuading chorus girls and countesses:
This, father, the last confidence you spoke.
In my twentieth year your old wounds woke
As cancer. Lodging under the same roof
Death was a visitor who hung about,
Strewing the house with pills and bandages,
Till he chose to put your spirit out.

Though they overslept the sequence of events
Which ended with the ambulance outside,
You lingering in the hall, your bowels on fire,
Tears in your eyes, and all your medals spent,
I summon girls who packed at last and went
Underground with you. Their souls again on hire,
Now those lost wives as recreated brides
Take shape before me, materialise.
On the verge of light and happy legend
They lift their skirts like blinds across your eyes.

By the early 1970s the Troubles were contorting our community. Occasionally I wondered what my father, an Englishman and an old soldier, would have made of it all. In the first stanza of 'Wounds', his memories of the trenches serve as a lens that may provide some kind of perspective. The second stanza confronts three contemporary atrocities.

Wounds

Here are two pictures from my father's head –
I have kept them like secrets until now:
First, the Ulster Division at the Somme
Going over the top with 'Fuck the Pope!'
'No Surrender!': a boy about to die,
Screaming 'Give 'em one for the Shankill!'
'Wilder than Gurkhas' were my father's words
Of admiration and bewilderment.
Next comes the London Scottish padre
Resettling kilts with his swagger-stick,
With a stylish backhand and a prayer.
Over a landscape of dead buttocks
My father followed him for fifty years.
At last, a belated casualty,
He said – lead traces flaring till they hurt –
'I am dying for King and country, slowly.'
I touched his hand, his thin head I touched.

Now, with military honours of a kind,
With his badges, his medals like rainbows,
His spinning compass, I bury beside him
Three teenage soldiers, bellies full of
Bullets and Irish beer, their flies undone.
A packet of Woodbines I throw in,
A lucifer, the Sacred Heart of Jesus
Paralysed as heavy guns put out
The night-light in a nursery for ever;
Also a bus-conductor's uniform –
He collapsed beside his carpet-slippers
Without a murmur, shot through the head
By a shivering boy who wandered in

Before they could turn the television down
Or tidy away the supper dishes.
To the children, to a bewildered wife,
I think 'Sorry Missus' was what he said.

I have loved Edward Thomas's poetry since my student days. I found
the next poem in his war diary and very lightly re-arranged his words. It is
almost a 'found poem'. It makes complete sense that, despite the mayhem
around him, Thomas remains attentive to the beauties of the natural world.
He was killed at the battle of Arras in April 1917. The one hundred and forty
poems he wrote in the last two years of his life are a miracle.

Edward Thomas's War Diary

1 January-8 April, 1917

One night in the trenches
You dreamed you were at home
And couldn't stay to tea,
Then woke where shell holes
Filled with bloodstained water,

Where empty beer bottles
Littered the barbed wire – still
Wondering why there sang
No thrushes in all that
Hazel, ash and dogwood,

Your eye on what remained –
Light spangling through a hole
In the cathedral wall
And the little conical
Summer house among trees.

Green feathers of yarrow
Were just fledging the sods
Of your dugout when you
Skirted the danger zone
To draw panoramas,

To receive larks singing
Like a letter from home
Posted in No Man's Land
Where one frantic bat seemed
A piece of burnt paper.

Generally regarded as the finest poet of the Second World War, Keith Douglas continues the great tradition of Owen and Sassoon, Rosenberg and Edward Thomas. In his poem 'Desert Flowers' Douglas apostrophises Isaac Rosenberg: 'Rosenberg, I only repeat what you were saying'. My poem 'Bog Cotton' echoes 'Desert Flowers' (beginning with the title) and ends with a reference to one of Rosenberg's masterpieces, 'Break of Day in the Trenches'.

Bog Cotton

Let me make room for bog cotton, a desert flower –
Keith Douglas, I nearly repeat what you were saying
When you apostrophised the poppies of Flanders
And the death of poetry there: that was in Egypt
Among the sandy soldiers of another war.

(It hangs on by a thread, denser than thistledown,
Reluctant to fly, a weather vane that traces
The flow of cloud shadow over monotonous bog –
And useless too, though it might well bring to mind
The plumpness of pillows, the staunching of wounds,

Rags torn from a petticoat and soaked in water
And tied to the bushes around some holy well
As though to make a hospital of the landscape –
Cures and medicines as far as the horizon
Which nobody harvests except with the eye.)

You saw that beyond the thirstier desert flowers
There fell hundreds of thousands of poppy petals
Magnified to blood stains by the middle distance
Or through the still unfocused sights of a rifle –
And Isaac Rosenberg wore one behind his ear.

In 'The War Poets' I mythologise the deaths of four poets. Keith Douglas was killed in the Normandy landing: a shrapnel fragment pierced the top of his skull. Rupert Brooke died from an infection caused by an insect bite. Edward Thomas was killed by shell-blast. Wilfred Owen died a week before the Armistice. These sad facts are only hinted at and do not distract from their symbolic suggestiveness. In no way documentary, the poem is not without hope but acknowledges between the lines that that hope is in vain.

The War Poets

Unmarked were the bodies of the soldier-poets
For shrapnel opened up again the fontanel
Like a hailstone melting towards deep water
At the bottom of a well, or a mosquito
Balancing its tiny shadow above the lip.

It was rushes of air that took the breath away
As though curtains were drawn suddenly aside
And darkness streamed into the dormitory
Where everybody talked about the war ending
And always it would be the last week of the war.

My father was brought up in Thirsk Road off Clapham Common. There were several family stories about his mother's mysterious gifts. In 'Second Sight' the home front becomes psychologically entangled with the distant battlefield and my own search for English roots. I never met my grandmother. I have a fuzzy photograph of her in a garden, dumpy and gentle beside my grandfather who was a journeyman carpenter.

Second Sight

My father's mother had the second sight.
Flanders began at the kitchen window –
The mangle rusting in No Man's Land, gas
Turning the antimacassars yellow
When it blew the wrong way from the salient.

In bandages, on crutches, reaching home
Before his letters, my father used to find
The front door on the latch, his bed airing.
'I watched my son going over the top.
He was carrying flowers out of the smoke.'

I have brought the *Pocket Guide to London*,
My *Map of the Underground*, an address –
A lover looking for somewhere to live,
A ghost among ghosts of aunts and uncles
Who crowd around me to give directions.

Where is my father's house, where my father?
If I could walk in on my grandmother
She'd see right through me and the hallway
And the miles of cloud and sky to Ireland.
'You have crossed the water to visit me.'

   I am pleased that 'The Kilt' manages to be a love poem as well as an
account of my father's nightmare (a recurring one). My twin and I slept in
the next bedroom to his. He seemed happy to tell us about the dream.
He never expressed remorse for the men he had killed.

The Kilt

I waken you out of your nightmare as I wakened
My father when he was stabbing a tubby German
Who pleaded and wriggled in the back bedroom.

He had killed him in real life and in real life had killed
Lice by sliding along the pleats a sizzling bayonet
So that his kilt unravelled when he was advancing.

You pick up the stitches and with needle and thread
Accompany him out of the grave and into battle,
Your arms full of material and his nakedness.

In Belfast returning wounded soldiers could find themselves in danger from the exuberance of their loyal supporters. To this day the wearing of the Remembrance Day poppy continues to be a contentious issue that divides Catholics and Protestants. I intend the 'poppies' that pile up at the end of the first four lines to express anger, sorrow, impatience, despair. In the next poem 'A Poppy' I give the symbolic flower space to breathe and grow, with a little help from Homer and Virgil.

Poppies

i

Some people tried to stop other people wearing poppies
And ripped them from lapels as though uprooting poppies
From Flanders fields, but the others hid inside their poppies
Razor blades and added to their poppies more red poppies.

ii

In Royal Avenue they tossed in the air with so much joy
Returning wounded soldiers, their stitches burst for joy.

A Poppy

When millions march into the mincing machine
An image from Homer picks out the individual
Tommy and the doughboy in his doughboy helmet:
'Lolling to one side like a poppy in a garden
Weighed down by its seed capsule and rainwater,
His head drooped under the heavy, crestfallen
Helmet' (an image Virgil steals – *lasso papavera
Collo* – and so do I), and so Gorgythion dies,
And the poppy that sheds its flower-heads in a day
Grows in one summer four hundred more, which means
Two thousand petals overlapping as though to make
A cape for the corn-goddess or a soldier's soul.

My wife and I have visited the battlefields and war cemeteries of northern France three times. I want the shape of 'The War Graves' to suggest the neat rows envisaged by the great architect, Edwin Lutyens, a poet in his way, a profound elegist. The poem begins in dusty St Quentin Cathedral and by the third stanza is taking in the tens of thousands of white headstones and the graves tended by French gardeners. At Agny, the little cemetery where Edward Thomas is buried, my wife wrote his exquisite quatrain 'Thaw' in the visitors' book. That day rooks were cawing. There are rooks in his poem.

The War Graves

The exhausted cathedral reaches nowhere near the sky
As though behind its buttresses wounded angels
Snooze in a halfway house of gargoyles, rainwater
By the mouthful, broken wings among pigeons' wings.

There will be no end to clearing up after the war
And only an imaginary harvest-home where once
The Germans drilled holes for dynamite, for fieldmice
To smuggle seeds and sow them inside these columns.

The headstones wipe out the horizon like a blizzard
And we can see no farther than the day they died,
As though all of them died together on the same day
And the war was that single momentous explosion.

Mothers and widows pruned these roses yesterday,
It seems, planted sweet william and mowed the lawn
After consultations with the dead, heads meeting
Over this year's seed catalogues and packets of seeds.

Around the shell holes not one poppy has appeared,
No symbolic flora, only the tiny whitish flowers
No one remembers the names of in time, brookweed
And fairy flax, say, lamb's lettuce and penny-cress.

In mine craters so vast they are called after cities
Violets thrive, as though strewn by each cataclysm
To sweeten the atmosphere and conceal death's smell
With a perfume that vanishes as soon as it is found.

At the Canadian front line permanent sandbags
And duckboards admit us to the underworld, and then
With the beavers we surface for long enough to hear
The huge lamentations of the wounded caribou.

Old pals in the visitors' book at Railway Hollow
Have scribbled 'The severest spot. The lads did well'
'We came to remember', and the woodpigeons too
Call from the wood and all the way from Accrington.

I don't know how Rifleman Parfitt, Corporal Vance,
Private Costello of the Duke of Wellington's,
Driver Chapman, Topping, Atkinson, Duckworth,
Dorrell, Wood come to be written in my diary.

For as high as we can reach we touch-read the names
Of the disappeared, and shut our eyes and listen to
Finches' chitters and a blackbird's apprehensive cry
Accompanying Charles Sorley's monumental sonnet.

We describe the comet at Edward Thomas's grave
And, because he was a fisherman, that headlong
Motionless deflection looks like a fisherman's fly,
Two or three white after-feathers overlapping.

Geese on sentry duty, lambs, a clattering freight train
And a village graveyard encompass Wilfred Owen's
Allotment, and there we pick from a nettle bed
One celandine each, the flower that outwits winter.

   Some of the most heartbreaking pictures to come out of the trenches are
of tormented horses struggling to escape the clutching mud (especially at
Passchendaele). Homer was clearly a lover of horses.

The Horses

For all of the horses butchered on the battlefield,
Shell-shocked, tripping up over their own intestines,
Drowning in the mud, the best war memorial
Is in Homer: two horses that refuse to budge

Despite threats and sweet-talk and the whistling whip,
Immovable as a tombstone, their heads drooping
In front of the streamlined motionless chariot,
Hot tears spilling from their eyelids onto the ground
Because they are still in mourning for Patroclus
Their charioteer, their shiny manes bedraggled
Under the yoke pads on either side of the yoke.

Based on episodes from *Edmund Blunden* by Barry Webb, 'Poetry'
explores the possibility of some kind of sodality of the imagination. Though
rooted in the daily life of the soldier poets, the best war poetry reaches
out beyond the confines of the trenches to, potentially, the whole world.
Incidentally, I sometimes wonder if my father ever shared a Woodbine or a
mug of tea with one of the Great War poets.

Poetry

When he was billeted in a ruined house in Arras
And found a hole in the wall beside his bed
And, rummaging inside, his hand rested on *Keats*
By Edward Thomas, did Edmund Blunden unearth
A volume which 'the tall, Shelley-like figure'
Gathering up for the last time his latherbrush,
Razor, towel, comb, cardigan, cap comforter,
Water bottle, socks, gas mask, great coat, rifle
And bayonet, hurrying out of the same building
To join his men and march into battle, left
Behind him like a gift, the author's own copy?
When Thomas Hardy died his widow gave Blunden
As a memento of many visits to Max Gate
His treasured copy of Edward Thomas's *Poems*.

There's a suite of seven short war poems in my eighth collection *Snow
Water*. I include three of them here. In yet another poem about Edward
Thomas I echo the breathtaking last line of 'Adlestrop'. In 'Pipistrelle' I
imagine a strange pet for a terribly wounded soldier. 'Harmonica' is my
favourite poem out of all my work. When I brought back from school a
harmonica, my father picked it up and started to play it quite well. I had
never heard him play anything before. During lulls in the fighting he and
his mates had taught themselves to play harmonicas. For years I had wanted

to write about this. Then in a study of early Greek philosophers I read about Anaximenes who believed that air was the basis of all creation. He breathed life into my memory. Every reader can choose his or her music-hall song. The one I hear in my head is 'Tipperary'.

Edward Thomas's Poem

i

I couldn't make out the minuscule handwriting
In the notebook the size of his palm and crinkled
Like an origami quim by shell-blast that stopped
His pocket watch at death. I couldn't read the poem.

ii

From where he lay he could hear the skylark's
Skyward exultation, a chaffinch to his left
Fidgeting among the fallen branches,
Then all the birds of the Western Front.

iii

The nature poet turned into a war poet as if
He could cure death with the rub of a dock leaf.
PIPISTRELLE

They kept him alive for years in warm water,
The soldier who had lost his skin.
                                    At night
He was visited by the wounded bat
He had unfrozen after Passchendaele,

Locking its heels under his forefinger
And whispering into the mousy fur.

Before letting the pipistrelle flicker
Above his summery pool and tipple there,

He spread the wing-hand, elbow to thumb.
The membrane felt like a poppy petal.

Harmonica

A Tommy drops his harmonica in No Man's Land.
My dad like old Anaximenes breathes in and out
Through the holes and reeds and finds this melody.

Our souls are air. They hold us together. Listen.
A music-hall favourite lasts until the end of time.
My dad is playing it. His breath contains the world.

The wind is playing an orchestra of harmonicas.

I had failed for years to track down the citation for my father's Military
Cross. I mentioned this in an article I wrote for the *Irish Times*. Out of the
blue, a reader sent me an address to which I posted off a stamped addressed
envelope and a cheque for four pounds. When the citation arrived, I wept.
I was flabbergasted by how brave my father had been. Without changing a
word I divided the citation into ten roughly twelve-syllable lines and added
a few lines of my own at the beginning and the end. It is nearly a 'found'
sonnet. That was the best four pounds I have ever spent.

Citation

It is like a poem. It is better than a poem,
The citation for my father's Military Cross
Dividing itself up into lines like this: 'For
Conspicuous gallantry and devotion to duty
In leading the waves of his company in a raid
And being the first to enter both objectives
In spite of a severe shrapnel wound in the thigh.
After killing several of the enemy himself,
He directed the fire of his Lewis gunners
And rifle bombers on to a working party
Of over 100 of the enemy and controlled
The mopping-up of the enemy dug-outs.'
Kept alive by his war-cry and momentum,
I shiver behind him on the fire-step.

To mark the centenary of the Great War, Carol Ann Duffy asked some poets to choose a piece of writing from the conflict that moved them, and then to write a poem in response to it. I chose a letter quoted in Thomas McAlindon's superb family memoir *Two Brothers Two Wars*. To match the simple beauty of this letter from his uncle Tom I enlisted Homer. My poem was included in Duffy's anthology *1914: Poetry Remembers*. Tom McAlindon served in the Royal Irish Rifles.

'We had a young volunteer here called Bobbie Kernaghan. He said he was seventeen but looked about fifteen to me. He was just out and so keen to get at the Germans, they had killed his favourite uncle. He was from Balfour Street in Belfast and said it's a small world, a neighbour of his was an Annie O'Hagan from the Mounties. Do you know her? I straightened his pack and checked his rifle (everything we have and wear is plastered with mud) before we went up and over on the 9th. We had hardly gone ten yards when he got it in the chest. He looked like a schoolboy asleep when they brought him in and laid him down. He lay covered over in the bottom of the trench for a few days. Every time I passed him I thought of when I was seventeen and of the nine years I've had since then. You get very callous here after a while, you simply have to, but this lad's death got through all my callousness. The Divisional Commander inspected us this morning and congratulated us on our "great work at Ovillers". Great!'

Boy-Soldier

The spear-point pierces his tender neck.
His armour clatters as he hits the ground.
Blood soaks his hair, bonny as the Graces',
Braids held in place by gold and silver bands.
Think of a smallholder who rears a sapling
In a beauty spot a burn burbles through
(You can hear its music close to your home)
Milky blossoms quivering in the breeze.
A spring blizzard blows in from nowhere
And uproots it, laying its branches out.
Thus Euphorbus, the son of Pantheus,
A boy-soldier – the London Scottish, say,
The Inniskillings, the Duke of Wellington's –
Was killed and despoiled by Menelaus.

I didn't really believe my father's story about Ronald Colman until I found Colman's name in the archive of the London Scottish.

Ronald Colman

My dad served with Ronald Colman in the Great War
And laughed at his daydream of Hollywood stardom.
London-Scottish kilts looked frumpish after battle,
Blood, mud and shit bespattering handsome knees.
My dad lost all his teeth before he was twenty
And envied Ronald Colman's spectacular smile.
He watched him trimming his moustache in cold tea
At a cracked mirror, a thin black line his trademark.
Wounded at Messines – shrapnel in his ankle –
He tried in his films to cover up his limp – *Beau
Geste, Lost Horizon* – my dad would go to see them all.
Did he share a last Woodbine with Ronald Colman
Standing on the firestep, about to go their separate
Ways, over the top, into No Man's Land, and fame?

My father was seriously wounded at the terrible battle of High Wood. I end this short poem by quoting the last two lines of Book Four of the *Iliad*. For obvious reasons I have changed 'dust' to 'mud'.

At High Wood

I picture my gentle dad at High Wood
Lying wounded among the splintered trees
And unburied dead, some of them his mates,
Some his victims, shot and bayoneted:
*Many Trojans and Achaeans fell that day
And lay side by side, faces in the mud.*

Homer sometimes makes the horrors of the battlefield seem even worse by using similes that are painful reminders of home and everyday life.

Lunch

i

Missiles find their mark,
On both sides soldiers fall
(Mutual wounds) but
The Greeks break through
At that time of day
When the woodcutter,
His arms exhausted
From chopping trees,
His stomach rumbling,
Prepares his lunch.

ii

Field-kitchen smells,
Memories of home
Between explosions –
Dad, can that be you
Rattling your mess tin
And bellyaching
About the bully beef
As the Germans advance?
Here is an apple
Wrapped in tranquility.

In Newtownards, war veterans grew so impatient over the long-delayed war memorial, they made out of snow their own cenotaph and snowman soldier. Some memorials are profound and poetic – the tomb of the unknown warrior, Edwin Lutyens' cenotaph and his Thiepval Memorial to the Missing of the Somme. Inadvertently, the old soldiers of Newtownards matched these sorrowful masterworks with their own spontaneous monument that was soon to melt.

The Cenotaph

They couldn't wait to remember and improvised
A cenotaph of snow and a snowman soldier,
Inscribing 'Lest We Forget' with handfuls of stones.

I want to give my gentle, courageous, reticent father the last word.

Anniversary

January 12, 1996

He would have been a hundred today, my father,
So I write to him in the trenches and describe
How he lifts with tongs from the brazier an ember
And in its glow reads my words and sets them aside.

Michael Longley: Three new poems

The Starlings

Sitting up against a sea wall,
Eating fish and chips, we count
The starlings, a dozen or so
Swaggering opportunists
Unexpected on the shingle.
Shall we throw them leftovers,
Dear brother? Greasy fingers.
Spangled iridescences.
Is this Bangor or Ballyholme?
A blink and they attract thousands
And thousands more starlings, a shape-
Changing bird-cloud, shitlegs
Sky-dancing. No collisions.
Wherever you are, Peter,
Can you spot on your radar
Angels? They're starlings really,
Heavenly riffraff flocking
Before they flap down to roost.

The Trilobite

for Bob Kennedy

Thank you for the trilobite,
Its four hundred million years
(Approximately) parcelled
With tissue paper and two
Elastic bands, carefully.
Set free by your hammer blow
From the muddy blackness
Of deep Ordovician seas,
It finds its way in sunlight
To Carrigskeewaun, eyeless
At the fireside among bleached
Bones and raven feathers.

The Magnifying Glass

for Fleur Adcock at 80

i

You gave me a gilded magnifying glass
For scrutinising the hearts of wild flowers
(Which I did, kneeling in water-meadows).
In the handle a paper-knife's concealed
For opening occasional letters from you.
Now that we're both shortsighted, Fleur, the lens
Enlarges your dwindling classicist's script.

ii

Dear Fleur, over the years we have signed off
Ornithologically: the East Finchley robins
And wrens and blue tits significant news,
My census of whooper swans and waders
From the wind and rain of Carrigskeewaun.
We've been out in the fields all our lives, heads
Down, looking on the ground for larks' nests.

Josephine Balmer

Michael Longley: *The Stairwell* (Cape Poetry, 2014)

'I have been thinking about the music for my funeral,' announces Michael Longley in the opening, eponymous poem to his entrancing new collection, *The Stairwell*. Such musings on mortality will come as no surprise to readers of Longley's previous nine volumes which have long rattled with the skeletons of the dead; Homeric warriors and doomed Ovidian shape-shifters jostling for position amongst the poet's lost friends, colleagues and family. But as in Longley's previous, acclaimed volume, 2011's *A Hundred Doors*, *The Stairwell* finds the now seventy-five year-old poet increasingly contemplating his own demise. So where 'The New Window', from *A Hundred Doors*, saw Longley 'sitting up in bed with binoculars' to 'scan/ My final resting place at Dooaghtry', here 'Ashes':

> Takes me along the perimeter fencing
> To where I want my ashes wind-scattered.
> ('Ashes')

There are other echoes of Longley's previous work here too. As in *A Hundred Doors* or *The Weather in Japan* (2000) and *Snow Water* (2004), a sequence of poems, exquisitely introduced by the contemplation that returning Tommies introduced the lizard orchid to Britain ('ribbons/ For widow hats'), celebrates his own father's active service in the Great War, the firsthand accounts passed on to Longley which have enriched his poetry since 'In Memoriam' from his 1969 debut collection, *No Continuing City* (see Longley's own discussion of such poems elsewhere in this issue). In *The Stairwell*, Longley senior remembers Passchendaele 'where men and horses drowned in mud'('Mud Turf') or in 'Ronald Colman' laughs at his fellow soldier's 'daydream of Hollywood stardom' (if later going to see all his films). Longley's mentor war poets, Edward Thomas and Ivor Gurney, the former a Longley regular since 1976's *Man Lying On A Wall*, also make a brief but compelling reappearance in 'Insomnia'. Here, in one of his trademark lightning-bright imaginative leaps between past and present, a sleepless Longley, mind-walking through his beloved County Mayo tracks, thinks of Edward's widow Helen who:

> took Ivor Gurney's hand
> When he was miles away from Gloucestershire

And sanity, and on Edward's county map
Guided his lonely finger down the lanes.
You are like Helen Thomas. Take my hand.
                              ('Insomnia')

Such poems, in turn, usher in another recurring Longley trope, his always outstanding use of ancient epic to underscore the universal horror of total war. But in *The Stairwell* he moves away from Homer's warrior heroes to the lesser-known foot soldiers who flit like ghosts through the *Iliad*. For example, there is Euphorbus in the perfect sonnet of 'Boy-Soldier' whose:

    armour clatters as he hits the ground.
Blood soaks his hair, bonny as the Graces',
Braids held in place by gold and silver bands....
A boy-soldier – the London Scottish, say,
The Inniskillings, the Duke of Wellington's –
Was killed and despoiled by Menelaus.
                              ('Boy-Soldier')

Elsewhere Idomeneus, from *A Hundred Doors'* 'Old Soldiers', returns, yet now Longley's surgical eye homes in on one of the Cretan warrior's victims, the otherwise unknown Trojan Erymas, as:

    the spear penetrates the brain
And splits the white bones, and the teeth
Blow out and from the eye-sockets
Blood squirts...
    ('Face')

Homer, Longley complains, 'gets no nearer than this/ To the anonymous Tommy'. But as in Alice Oswald's 2011 *Memorial*, Longley's own deft manipulation of Homer's original gives these grey shades substance. In 'Boy-Soldier', he urges us to think of Euphorbus as 'a smallholder':

    who rears a sapling
In a beauty spot a burn burbles through
(You can hear its music close to your home)
                              ('Boy-Soldier')

This final unassuming parenthesis lies at the core of Longley's poetic method, revealing the skill – almost casual in its inclusivity – with which he connects us to the ancient world. And so in 'Grasshoppers' the Homeric armies become 'The old fellas/ Above Troy's gate / Demobbed by age'. In 'The Tin Noses Shop', Longley transforms, like an alchemist, the dull metal of the soldiers' crude prosthetics into Agamemnon's mask, 'eyebrow and eyelids/ Hammered out of gold.' In doing so, he peels back the layers of dust and scholarly convention to lay bare the universality of Homer's ancient archetypes. At the same time Longley offers the poet's new penetrating readings of classic works, as incisive as any professor's monograph. As he explains in his illuminating 2009 essay 'Lapsed Classicist', 'I have been Homer-haunted for fifty years'.

Above all, though, Longley is a poet not just of war and death but grief. More than any, he understands the full fury of its chaotic force which renders even the great warrior Achilles like 'a lion, heartbroken when he finds/ His neglected cubs snatched from their thicket' ('The Lion'). Part Two of *The Stairwell* presents a superb series of elegies for what must be one of the hardest losses to bear, that of the poet's twin, his brother Peter. Here, again, Homer provides a means to 'wail in excruciating lamentation', as Longley recasts himself as Achilles mourning his beloved Patroclus ('a double, a twin'), while the process of grieving becomes Patroclus' funeral games from *Iliad* Book 23. Now the sibling quarrels of the Longleys' boyhood become entwined with epic conflict:

We were combatants from the start. Our dad
Bought us boxing gloves when we were ten –
Champions like Euryalus, say, or Epeius
Of wooden-horse fame....

('The Boxers')

These intertexual shifts might at first glance seem distancing to those who, like Peter, as we discover in 'The Alphabet', prefer practical metalwork to learning the Greek alphabet. Yet, as the sequence progresses, the boys' childhood acquires its own mythical, equally epic status. For instance, Homer's lion simile for Achilles is transmuted into 'the lion at Bellevue Zoo... Paws crossed, gazing out over Belfast Lough' ('The Lion'). And the slightly sad stallion manoeuvres of returning GIs, which the boys watch from behind a hawthorn in Bristow Park, are in their turn transformed into Achilles' 'wind-swift/ Horses'('The Stallion'). By the time the two are characterised as 'the twin Moliones/ Kteatos and Eurytos, Aktor's sons' in 'The Twins', it barely matters who these fairly minor mythical characters might have been; this is the universal language of loss, of those as close as:

Siamese twins, joined below the waist,
One grasping the reins for dear life,
The other whipping the horses to win,
Two souls, one well-balanced charioteer
Taking the trophy and this epitaph.

('The Twins')

As the reader arrives at 'The Birthday', and its bald opening statement
– 'This is our first birthday without you' – the pain of mourning becomes
almost unbearable. But, as ever, Longley's lightness of touch brings
us back to earth in a matter of lines: 'Have you been skinny-dipping at
Allaran' he enquires of his brother's ghost. And then, mentioning the
organic beetroots cooking for supper, he wonders: 'Will your pee be pink in
heaven?' Elsewhere the disappearance of one of Peter's cats just before his
death leads, via a translation from French of Gwen John's sweet but slight
evocation of a straying cat, to the revelation that:

The day of your funeral
In October sunshine
Milly, not the friendliest
Tabby, came back home.

('The Stray')

For in the middle of death, it seems, we are always in life. Even Longley's
own 'unassuming *nunc dimittis*' is contained within the poem 'Birth-Bed', as
he wakes in the bed in which his baby granddaughter has only recently been
born (this in turn counterbalances 'Deathbed' which the poet characterises
as a playground for swooping robins, his 'soul-birds'). Throughout *The
Stairwell*, grandchildren dance in and out of the lines – new-born Amelia
or toddler Maisie wondering during a power-cut 'Where is me?/ I have
disappeared' ('Haiku') or chattering to herself, 'her speech-melody/ A
waterlily budding' in 'Maisie at Dawn'. These births are offset by the deaths
not just of Longley's twin but of old friends and, poignantly, the children
of old friends, for whom Longley leaves 'unpicked/ One fragrant orchid
for her to kneel and sniff' ('Fragrant Orchid'). There are short elegies, too,
for Longley's 'fellow voyager' Seamus Heaney and his family. For like
Yeats, whom Longley considers the greatest poet of the English language
bar Shakespeare, Longley has become the supreme poet of old age, growing
in stature as he contemplates the ever-renewing cycles of decay and rebirth,
moving forward into the inevitable shadow of death.

At the centre of Longley's affirming poetry, is the solid earth of his own much-trodden patch of Mayo, the townland of Carrigskeewaun. Every inch of this, it seems, has been celebrated in his delicate verse until his readers come to feel that they, too, walk across it with the step of a local; its herons and otters, lakes and salt marsh, anemones and helleborines, the stoat 'Sucking oxygen through/ A hole in the throat', the lapwings that 'flap away over Lackakeely'. In 'The Birthday' it is this landscape that comforts the poet on his day without his twin – 'the sandpipers eyeing Dooaghtry / For a nesting place among the pebbles' or the choughs that flock 'high above their acrobatic/ Cliff face' – as he imagines Peter's ghost flitting across his own much-loved landscape ('Thank you for visiting Carrigskeewaun/ Don't twist your ankle in a rabbit hole'). And in 'The Duckboards', he movingly follows, with Peter, his father's ghost across the marshes, as past and present again elide:

> as though at Passchendaele
> Teetering on walkways that disappear
> As we follow behind him in the rain.
> ('The Duckboards')

Back in 'The Stairwell' , Longley is shaken from his reverie on his own demise by similar acts of remembrance. As his hostess takes him to inspect the lobby of her apartment building, suitably decorated for Halloween with 'cobwebby/ Skulls, dancing skeletons', he tests 'the perfect acoustic' of the poem's (and the collection's) title stairwell by whistling Great War songs – 'Over There', 'It's a Long, Long Way' and 'Keep the Home Fires burning' – 'as though for my father'. In return, he is rewarded by the reverberating sound of 'songbirds circling high up', instantly bringing to mind the birdsong of Edward Thomas' 'Adlestrop'. These echoes typify the soaring humanity of Longley's work as it reaches back into the far distant as well as the recent past with equal clarity, yet at the same time resonates within its own meticulously constructed present. As such, Longley is a poet not only of old age but of any age, all ages – one of our best to stand beside both Thomas and Yeats.

Hilary Davies

Walk here with me

Walk here with me. We do not know how long.
The braided waters cross the marsh beside Bomb Crater Pond.
Bullrushes sing by the causeway,
In the leafing copses. And through the air we hear
The tumble of the swallows, their high-cloud mewing.
The sun was all around us. O my darling
How in the harvest of our days we were
And on the swans' backs the pearls of life
Streamed.

        Now the water of your breath
Breaks in a rainbow over each moment
We walked together where the willows and alders
Stretch their arms heavenward
And the cormorants circle
Over the rowers – o so full of life! –
Beating into the future.
But here, see, my heart is hung on the hawthorn
For you with your stoop stride never
Never never will walk by my side
Along the sweet Lea river nor lift your head
To hear the geese cry keening, ever again.

Alison Brackenbury

Break from poppy collection, Liverpool Street

Plumed for the Household Cavalry
the young black bandsman, brass on knee,
told me he never learned to ride
before the Army. Bruised, astride
huge Irish hunters, he clung on –

So one small ploughboy, plumping for
the cavalry's ranks for his Great War,
who left the sucking clay of fields,
hay-loaded creak of wagon's wheels
found himself perched, sky-high, on Bess,
white, bony, older than the rest.
'Recruits', the bandsman told me, 'can't
pick and choose their favourite mount.'

The farm boy, his short legs like straw,
shivered in Egypt's sun before
their first charge. How would she keep up?
The trumpets shook the sweating troop,
then, as a shot-wise pheasant runs,
Bess spun, then galloped from the guns.

Pensioned

Yes, I saw Hezekiah Brown,
a tall man, stately, with one eye.
The shrapnel took it in the war,
the Great War. But he fought on, by
my grandfather, a gamekeeper
who would have shot him for a hare.

Fifty years on, he drove along
our village edge, his skewbald mare
hauling small scrap on a loose rein.
They stopped ten yards from the front door,
by wind-blown fuchsias, raspberries.
How had he learnt that Frank lived there?

And when we drove first to the sea,
my father gestured to a place
a green shelf by a small quarry,
quiet no man's land, sufficient space,
caravan, horse. Here Hezekiah
drove back to wife, high fire, then snored

like my grandfather, safe beneath
his Council roof. Fifty years more
we may hold mortgages, a car,
send others' sons to distant war,
swim heated seas, keep no room for
one van, cropped grass, now we are poor.

New Court, Cheltenham

Officers convalesced by coasts,
ratings shook here, inland, by train,
found iron beds, lawns. Before the house

changed into flats, its old wards lost,
one woman made this small museum.
She lined brass buttons up, of course,

photos where Germans grin, fat rats
swing proudly from their washing lines.
She built a trench. By sandbags' brown

I inch, along dry duckboards' slats.
The bulged bags block wet skies, the town.
Recruit, I squint. I hear their shout
for the first time. 'Keep your head down!'

Frances-Anne King

Pembrokeshire Quilt

1915

After the telegram arrived
she rolled out sky-blue satin cotton,
took softest lamb's-wool wadding –
recalling mountain rambles,
how they picked fleece from crevices
in stone walls, hedges, ditches,
how she taught him to card wool
to remove twigs and thistles.
Sunlight sparked her rows of threaded needles
in their scarlet velvet cushion
turning them to minute bayonets and lances.
She didn't need her templates,
the tailor's chalk moved smoothly
as if her hand had somehow
always known this journey.
A starfish medallion, two borders,
one of waves and shells,
one of flowers and fern fronds,
then acorns in each corner. Stars and spirals –
so many spirals, as if this emblem of eternity
might reel him in a fraction closer –
the child whose kingdom was an oak wood,
who came home at dusk
the smell of green a song on him;
the beach comber who collected ammonites,
egret's feathers, salt-washed wood
buffed smooth as bone in moonlight;
the boy who learned the constellations,
told her the stars' white shining
was already in the past.

When finished, she'd fold her quilt,
take it up the mountain to that place
where stone cromlechs covered
ancient warriors, where fields
and wooded valleys sloped down
to a gentian sea. Here she'd bury it –
in soil his bones would never lie in.

Terry Dammery

Cabbage Whites

Like drops of sunlight
incarnated souls
dappling the patch

She in an apron
face empty as her bowl
half aware as they drift

Scattered flowers
half forgotten thoughts
petals thrown at a wedding

Light as lint they were
the colour of truce
fragile as lost moments

And she remembered
watching their whimsy
those times shelling peas
in days before the men-folk went
leaving in their going the cabbage white

Sarah's Bucket

The room it was under the stairs
and you would hear the handle as it fell

Her hair was piled in a Victorian bun
grey as a wet November day

What she did was kept a secret
pointless words to drown the sounds

She lost her sweetheart at Passchendaele
his breath bubbling in the mud

And when she brought the bucket back
she would raise her apron to her eyes

As the cistern filled she'd sit and smoke
quiet as though she'd heard sad news

Perhaps she was thinking of her lover
those times when she saw the bubbles rise

Breakwaters

She told me how the breakwaters stepped like decades along the coast
their footings in another century, deep below the foaming surf

That up on the cliffs fresh faced maidens promenaded their hems
their gowns a lot like hers
while a band played and blazered beaus tipped their boaters to the sun

How, down along the beach the bladderwrack waved from the depths
dark shadows that patterned the shallows in the low of the springs

And how the cormorants dived under the crests as thunder rolled
like long days of shelling, heavy from a land across the channel sea

She told of the breakwaters, like weathered spines, tracking up the shingle
climbing the beach out of the weed covered rocks that traced the shore

She told, too, that maids aged to spinsters, dry like flotsam on the tide-line
crochet hooks caught in the lace, parasols gone to parapluies

How there'd been twelve hours of sunshine bleaching the cliffs of the strait
and a scream of merlins out of the glare
as terns fell from the sky like shot planes, smashing the glass of a summer sea

But it was the breakwaters, the survivors, she always came back to
Calming the storms, stilling the waters
their structures emerging and surfacing, wave after wave
born out of function, like children of Telford, their iron the form-work of fate

N. S. Thompson

Gurney: At The Front

Was it a mine? To him Aladdin's cave
    More like,
Or really like a mine shaft, candle lit.
    So in he crawled

And found the men were Welsh, pit men, and felt
    That much
At home; immediately, rather than speak,
    They fell to song

And it was music to his soul, the Celt
    In him,
And – singing with them – felt so less the freak
    He had so long…

Now vacantly in these asylum walls,
    So smooth,
He asks whatever happened to the prop
    That held him up

With those men crouched like animals in stalls
    Of straw
And felt the good fatigue that let him drop
    Like wine into a cup…

He never felt like that again,
    That first
Night he experienced the tingling thrill
    With men unharmed

Who triumphed over bitter wind and rain
    And hail
Of bullets and bombs' thunder, which their still
    Strong voices calmed…

… Yes, I remember all the thrill it gave
    Me there
As now I live a freak show in the pit
    In which life stalled.

John Greening

The Lost Boys

It's 1916. First day of the Somme.
You're out for stand-to, staring into smoke.
Behind you is a field that runs back home.

In front of you are shell-holes, craters. Come!
The piper pipes you; there's his magic cloak.
It's 1916. First day of the Somme.

They walked you here (all roads lead to Bapaume)
Through mazes, puzzles, Lewis Carroll jokes
(Behind you is a field that runs back home)

And left you with some bones, a hat, a drum,
To dream with fairylights and brownie folk.
It's 1916. First day of the Somme.

The story's ending. Nurse begins to hum.
She'll tuck you up; now there's a sheet to stroke.
Behind you is a field that runs back home.

And soon you'll reach the point where you fall dumb
And happy ever after. Soon, with luck.
It's 1916. First day of the Somme.
Behind you is a field that runs back home.

Artillery Wood

to Francis Ledwidge

We did not come to find your 'little grave',
although it has a name, a number too;
it's just the first one that we found to show
these youngsters off the ferry. It would give
them some idea. But there you were, the lad
who wrote his tender verses and was hit
while laying duckboards through the mud and heat
of Pilckem Ridge. Here Ledwidge has been laid
in one of eight neat rows. Hard to believe it.
Another beat in someone else's line
of blank white verse. Except by heart, unknown,
this twenty-year-old smiling Irish private.

Jane Lovell

Transport Ship SS Keresaspa, December 1918

We steamed out from the mist
and chill of Liberty's shadow,
a cargo of four hundred mules and horses
bound for France.

Uncertain in the rising shift and tilt
they scuffed their hooves,
rooted in the half-dark for a streak of sky;
some say, smelt the barreling storm.

Nine days in, it hit,
towering above the ship,
shattering the sheds, hurling rafts
and lifeboats to the black Atlantic.

Flung about with every trough and swell
we clambered below,
heard through the storm's roar
the horses' frantic clamour.

We lost fifty-three that night,
thrown from stalls, piled in a turmoil
of shanks and halters,
their great chests heaving,

or floundering above,
hooves skidding loose over decks,
tangling in stanchions and winches.

Some were thrown wild-eyed and bucking
into slabs of ocean,
others stumbled into hatches;
legs and spines snapped like hazel.

Lights down and the wind driving waves
into cliffs of water,
wreckage strewn in all directions,
we did what we could.

Late morning, gales eased,
the dead were hoisted overboard.

We stared into the yearning deep
remembering the one that jumped
arcing into the wind, mane stiff with salt,
eyes pinned on the horizon.

Shell

Imagine this in slow motion
and silence: a shell dragging in its wake
across a land of wire and mud
the moiling sky,

a time-lapse sky, the thin tinkering
of larks, starlings sucked in
black and twisted fragments
against cloud,

the whisper of the pipe plucked
from his hand, hiss and pop of air
stretching cell and cavity, belly
blown-out like a bag.

He lands on scags of wire,
pressure-drop sapping capilliary,
artery, filling ear and lung,
and is gone.

Then roar and blast and shout,
slugging of boots through mud,
sky-rip brightness and slam
of impact,

rising in a windstorm,
the scream of shells,
of the horse
with ruptured eyes,

the deafening shudder
of life stilled...

and then the quietest sound
ghosting in from another world,
the folding and unfolding
of linen, of letters

of clean, white days billowing
before rain,
of measured words,
his last.

Mario Petrucci

(for the fallen)

step through now

and gently – step through that door
a life is: the heat of noon behind you

walk the cool marble of a life of labour
– breathe easy now – that struggle

over – outside the light dims – go
in – she waits for you where pain is

a memory struggled for – she is waiting
there in the ease of two hearts grown

to one shape – take your place now
beside her: this house is bright with love

and in the fields your hosts of kin
expect you – we will follow – for us

it is a long road to follow – but for you
the smallest step: as a child vanished in

crowds leaps into the arms of its mother
or a soldier thought lost in the wars

returns down the familiar path and as
recognition clamours the fields

steps under the childhood fig tree
to sit in its fruit-bearing shade

Stuart Henson

Wait

(Henry Williamson, Stiffkey, Norfolk, 1938)

Out of the dark they speak, voices like owls',
the poets calling each to each again,
distinct yet coded: Thomas through the rain's
mesh, something akin to the wind howling
across the salt marsh, strangulated vowels
scarcely distinguishable though he strains
to separate the truth, the praise, the pain,
from nature's chaos where his last hope drowns.

Fasces and Eagles and the ruse of peace;
the politics too little and too late...
He lies all night beside his shotgun, wild-eyed,
begging old comrades for a quick release.
And death holds out the hand he once denied
until one cries from woods near Arras, *Wait!*

Sue Mackrell

Nottingham Lace Market

Link, stitch, loop,
pass thread over,
pick up stitch,
wind around the bobbins,
keep the tension even.

Brain patterns locked into
mechanical action,
fingers following
pattern and predictability,
a locked web of synapses
triggering
repetitive thought
repetitive action,
compulsive responsibility,
a curse of control.

Neatened ends defy chaos,
a denial of casual carnage
life sustained by ritual
weight of lace, of fate.

I will weave so you will live,
each day marked by
three hexagonals of lattice,
curlicued leaves, picot links,
precise intricacy.

Postcards edged with Flemish lace
tell me you keep
your side of the bargain,
scalloped fleur de lis,
a bobbin lace of filmy flowers,
fine mesh filigree.

Link, stitch,loop,
pass thread over,
pick up stitch.
wind around the bobbins,
keep the tension even.

Westminster Bridge

How many times have you crossed this bridge
in three score years and ten?

You don't answer, haven't heard,
above the staccato tattoo
of your walking stick.
But I already know the answer:
beyond counting.

Big Ben strikes, and
Oranges and Lemons
Say the bells of St Clements,
London Bridge is falling down,
Falling down, falling down.

Your father, holding you tight
by the hand,
walking London streets by the mile.
Passing the Cenotaph,
he tells you to doff your cap,
wheezing still with the gas,
half-blinded on the Somme.

Turn Again Whittington,
Lord Mayor of London,
rhymes and stories passed
on and on,

Firewatching at St Paul's,
bombs and smogs,
a Pearly Queen aunt,
a costermonger uncle
bitten by a tarantula at Covent Garden,
stories of Fleet Street,
Borough Market, and Petticoat Lane.
street cries of *E'ening Stan'ard*
and *Any old Iron?*
ring in my ears
as I go up the *Apples and Pears*
to bed.

And on your last journey
we throw red roses over
Westminster Bridge.
petals scatter in the wake of a
pleasure boat,
'The Pride of London'.

Ring a ring a roses,
All fall down.

Games of Chance

Playing tag across a cobbled no man's land
marbles in a culvert, knock down ginger,
scabbed and picked knees a badge of honour.

Tossing a coin, king's head, king's shilling
a game of chance, third to light a cigarette.
a click of Russian roulette, a throw of dice.

Wounded, missing, died, wounded, missing survived,

Blind man's-buff, a line of men, hands on shoulders,
a game of piggy back for a dying man
pin the tail on the donkey scattered across the trench.

Fairground games, hit the rat with a hammer
a flea circus jumping across a bunk,
racing lice stubbed out with a woodbine.

Wounded, missing, died, wounded, missing, survived,

A game of chess plotting trenches,
pre-emptive Monopoly trading,
Piccadilly and Hellfire Corner,
Bomb Alley and Dead Man's Road.

Pontoon, the card game of choice,
get to 21, if you're lucky,
or a ticket to Blighty.

Wounded, missing, died, wounded, missing, survived,

Noughts and crosses.
Seven noughts, ten million men,
a multitude of crosses.

David Kuhrt

Henry

25.10.1880 – 26.6.1954

Through dog-fight, black-out, King and Country,
cloth cap raised to a lady, you traipsed five miles
from the Flatts to Lombard Street and back
to score a wage; a weekend Dig for Victory
on a little allotment.

Then Monday would come again; duty this time
done at De la Rue's. Ledger-entries penned, ink
well filled, your pocket wasn't. Just the job –
it helped, to see that theirs would be.
A perfect bird's-foot script,

this clipped wing was your stump of identity,
legging it fifty years to earn the nickel-plated
salver on our sideboard. And we little ones,
seeing it displayed, would remember
your father, out of Schleswig,

the Hun take-over a shame for the Dane. Loyal
to our crown, you passed through our scullery,
big, but timid before the indigenous Lily
(grandma, your wife). My brother and I,
ready for smack bottoms,

you sat on the closet in the back yard, saying
High Anglican evensong. Lily, the Strict Baptist
inside, thinking this popery, we would watch,
get on with our porridge, as you trod back
to the kitchen sink to shave,

swishing the cut-throat over the strop, hitched
to the door-frame, thinking: God help us –
the thought of your son, my father, looping
the loop with a joy-stick up above, shot
down in his Spitfire

after the posting to Lossiemouth. Has it helped
to die like this, a safeguard against war-mongers
in Whitehall? As if love could not overcome
heredity; as if the footslog after Schleswig
were worth it.

The Trojan War Has Not Been Won

for Laurence James Kuhrt, shot down in his Spitfire

A shame if nostalgia grips a past not past;
  if premonition thinks duty proscribes
    a liberty to live.

Those splendid ends we shop for hang on family.
  Love's routine, revering ancestry,
    brings in the unborn.

These glories darken, spent,
  if King and Country expect
    the trench I am buried in
      defends imperial power.

Since when? The Trojan War
  has not been won! At stake
    is Helen's heritage. Let's rest
      in peace with this antiquity.

Richard Ormrod

September Sunflowers

They bow their great gold heads
upon the bodies of their stalks
as if in shame, or in final defeat
after a long bombardment, when victory
seemed in sight. All summer long
they proudly wooed the sun and won,
erect as an army of young men
in field upon field. Now
their round, flat faces are fallen
limp, sad, waiting for the thresher,
as if to say, 'It is finished. Done.'

Theirs are necessary deaths:
their oil will feed, lubricate, heal;
ploughed back into the soil
their remains, phoenix-like,
will resurrect again next year,
unlike the unquiet bones
of those buried in France
a century back—blackened,
scattered, eroded, shattered—
who are ploughed-up still in spring
or lying in acres of white stones.

Ruth O'Callaghan

Miss Hathaway Sweeps Her Path in Autumn 1916

i.m. of the women 'canaries' who suffered mental and physical problems due to the toxic chemicals they worked with in the factories

She sees they have scattered gold
where the gate once hung
to tempt her from the path

to tempt her to cross the cracks
they even placed a black cat
beyond the boundary

she knew safe. She will not sing
though they call her canary.
Her yellow hand plucks

a feather from the path to sweep
the gold to shelter by the blind
daffodils, bound since March

when they pretended dead – fallen
innocents in a time where diatribe
reigns and generals

remain at the rear. She recognises
each passing person's greeting
knowing the code:

a hand half-raised – the salute –
the head inclined to the left
– the warning –

or the nod which means she must leave
within the week. Speech
is not exchanged.

When he who comes with words lingers
where brambles guard the path
she will close the air

where the gate once hung. If the time
proves auspicious she will pluck
a snowdrop to light her way.

Lament

The wind brings the gas.
The soft wind from the south brings the gas.

The sun burns the men.
The ceaseless sun from the east burns the men.

The snow hides the dead.
The quiet snow from the north hides the dead.

The rain decays the bodies.
The constant rain from the west decays the bodies.

The wind brings the gas.
The soft wind from the south brings the gas.

Tony Roberts

Somme

He palmed the rouge
of his ten franc Marianne
and then in three weeks
when the huge
bombardment began
he worked it in his cheeks
to boost the confidence of his men.

The good Lord favoured neither her nor them.

Wendy Holborrow

Soldiers in the Snow

It is not our responsibility to find the absence…
we do not have to clarify the meaning of life.
                                                    Brecht

Sleet bluffed snow for a while
now it muffles with its whiteness
under deckle-edged leaden clouds.
The quietness of the snow –
its quilted silence – deadens
all sound until

a trudge of soldiers cuts the stillness
through a fold of eldritch fields.
They emit a core of confidence,

going faster through the blanketed world
as they hasten to avoid
another disaster, seeking revenge.

Purblind here, they should know
that an eye for an eye
makes everyone blind.

The snow that once lay like pure linen,
is turning to slush, like crushed sheets
from a turbulent sleep

or winding sheets, if these
are the unlucky ones
whose wives become widows.

The Widow

War does not determine who is right, only who is left.

Bertrand Russell

She sleeps the memories away, sweeps their terror
into her dreams from where they emerge
to urge her recollections.

Cold. She sits beside the flaming fire.
Above the sink her lone toothbrush
mocks her aloneness.

The last time she kissed him was
as if she were drinking the man, as if her thirst
could never be quenched,

but the stinking gin she drinks now
causes shifting splotches behind her shut eyes –
bursts of pain.

She has been a cuckquean to the army
who carelessly lose thousands of limbs
and lives.

Their promises and lies,
wormwood words
leave a bitter taste.

If only he could have drunk
the unguent of Prometheus to render him safe
against fire and weapons,

or that she could forever bathe
in the etherised waters
of Lethe.

Robert Stein

To His Patron

My dear Princess
I am hereby rejecting the commission
For 'something from Nature's realm'
To benefit the burghers, citizens and children of
The town of Hainburg an der Donau.

Instead, this Sunday, sharp at five o'clock
In the Old Square of Hainburg an der Donau
I will for 30 minutes by that clock
Pour ink over myself
That over the years has soured gradually in my study.

Please inform the good citizens
Of Hainburg an der Donau, their wives etc.
They are at liberty to stare into the ink and see
Soulfulness, waterfalls,
The bitterness of night, an exhortation,
The bottomless well or just ink, as they see fit.

I then promise to draw a ladder with the ink.
See: I do nothing out of love.
I hold my hand out to the moon
Only to feel the cold coming from it.
I scratch at it as I would scrabble up a cliff.
The ladder I'm sure will be a prized exhibit.

My esteemed Princess
While I walk away I shall be interested to hear
What the noble citizens of Hainburg an der Donau
More honestly think. My darkened back
Shall follow me dripping into the night.
Perhaps I shall smile again at that
White voluptuary the moon
Who can look down always unimpugned. Goodnight.

Peter Carpenter

Cricket on The Head

Tonbridge School, 1913

Maybe this practice game
    will go on forever –

keeper standing up, fielders
    walking in before

each delivery as per skipper's orders.
    Like clockwork. Summer's

a distant sundial in the rose garden,
    a bell for chapel, or just

us lot lolling in this heavenly shade,
    grass burns streaking the knees

of ironed whites. A half volley
    is played up to the man at mid on…

One more ball then Walshy
    will hand Goacher

his cap, stroll across
    to square leg, call 'over'.

Stuart Medland

The Piper

(to Sergeant-Piper Daniel Laidlaw)

Every man pulled up and over –

And despite himself – though
not by hand clasped onto wrist whose
hand is locked to wrist again at
its own turning of the key (the
lovers' knot of Brothers
in their Arms) but by the

Drone and skirl. The piper
walking forward already to his
missing-heartbeat, his own syncopate
and studied time, still managing his
jangle-limbed and loch-hauled

Bag of music, only yesterday
still struggling to be brought to
heel, though limp-leg and close-clinging
in his arms today and he exacting
every yearning strain of hearth, of glen and burn
and mist-soaked mountain for his trouble,

Un-returning to them
into thunderous cacophony and

At the heart of which not heard at all but for
three notes of All the Blue Bonnets Over the Border
in some unearthly lull with clearing smoke

And there upon a slight horizon,
playing only now to snatch up any
muddied heart left in a working body,
drag it homewards through yet one more
gangle-limbed and lungs-pressed-
into-moaning-music trench. Still

Up and over, lost in heather, deaf
to all but moor-birds piping on the brae.

Note:
Of the 2,500 unarmed pipers serving in the Scottish regiments through the Great
War, 500 were killed in action and some 600 wounded. Many new pieces of music
such as 'The Bloody Fields of Flanders' were composed by the pipers whilst
waiting in the trenches and often written only upon whatever came to hand. These
tunes, as documented on the recent BBC programme, Pipers of the Trenches, have
been painstakingly collected as part of a project undertaken by The Scottish Pipers
Association.

George

(for George Butterworth)

For Banks of Green Willow these
trenches of mud. For God-swelling

English and up-welling Maysong this
Antichrist music of shell and of scream.

For shock-stupid silence your silence.

Alongside this Bach-music, Beethoven-music,
each opus of Elgar, no body of work to stand
shoulder to shoulder, by Butterworth; George.

Ruth Smith

As Though He Still Slept Here

One summer day I walk into this high, square room,
starched towels on the washstand, a narrow bed,
long view of the gardens, curtains billowing
with each fetch of air. The boy slept here and then
the man between the same two palisades of brass.
The rug's original, nap gone, faint hints
of geometric flowers, crushed by the impress
of his lowered feet. The room has been arranged
as though he still slept here, as though the last thing
he took up was that copy of *The Field*, as though
he'd take his pen and dip it in the round silver inkpot
blotting words when they at last began to flow.
Books line the mantle shelf, the sort of thing
he might have read if he'd had time. A hip bath
has been brought in and placed beside the fire.
The coat was his. He's wearing it, fresh-shaven,
monocled, in the oval photograph. Off to the races
or a ball. But now there's not a single blond hair
left among the ranks of brushes in his dressing case.
When it came back from Loos, his mother laid it
open on the bed, before she locked the room.

Richard Greene

Corner Boys

They chew the stems of pipes, loiter
in the sweet smoke they make. I remember
sleeves folded and pinned, a pant leg sewed
off at the knee – this vividness unexplained.
Beside them, a blind accordionist
plays out-harbour songs for nickels and dimes.
Down a lane, a man with a barrow sells cod,
and along the harbour, cargo ships
and fishing boats crowd the coves
with enterprise and the sense of going
far. My grandmother urges me on: Ayre's,
Bowring's, Parker Monroe, Steele's – hats, shoes,
kitchen gear. For us, a day of errands.
Something of that stays in memory,
but also the men we pass, the ones whose years
came to little between armistice
and old age, all their private intentions
spent in the doing of a duty. They are gone
before I have any notion of who they are,
the last of the Blue Puttees, the men
of Beaumont Hamel, of Arras and Cambrai;
crutch-propped corner boys on Water Street,
backs to brick and stone, their salient
a length of pavement and a few small shops.

Peter Kahn

Ten Thousand Takers

after Bob Dylan

Ten seconds can be a barbell bearing two
thousand pounds across the thin crux of your throat.
Takers of what she said with her lips and her eyes
whose shade of brown sun-rised with the touch of your

tongues. Years puffing to an iron cloud of what you
were with words unbound from nicety's anchor.
All rank and un-showered. Nothing can fix the
broken windpipe of what no longer breathes.

Sunset Coming On

After Damon Albarn

Sunset is one death we can live with. The
coming apart of day, the black light turning

on. The sun's siblings spitting white. *The uh
oh* of tripped promises. The *cross-my-hearts, good*

Lord no's making tomorrow glow in the dark like today's
but a hazy inconvenience. Its reincarnation sure to be

the answer to the question we don't know how to ask.
Sunrise—the sky's jack-o-lantern trick goading us so

we'll get up even if yesterday blackened our eye so we can't
see. The sun powers up with the day. We stare forward

again. Stretch and shake the sleep from our crusted eyes.

Olive M. Ritch

H.M.S. Hampshire

(for the men who could not tell their stories)

In heavy seas, they heard sailors
shout as they clung to rafts and wreckage
on that June night in nineteen-sixteen;
                                                    soles
of fathers and sons champing
to scale the cliff face, feet
and hands already roughened
on the rocks of Marwick Head –
long used to scrambling from ledge
to ledge stealing seagulls' eggs.

At the cliff edge, men recalled
Lord Kitchener's command:
'Your country needs YOU'.
But not on that June night,
said Grandad, an official
turned us away, saying:
'everything's under control'.

The next day, bodies
                        were brought to land.

Eric Morgan

The Battle of Jutland

HMS Defence. The first to go.
The Admiral's blazoned flag
had led the squadron, four ironclads,
thick and trudging, in the channel
between Beatty's pride and the Huns of Jutland.
Smoke enough to choke the North Sea –
Jellicoe grumbled at the belching.
Then the Jerries' pinpoint broadsides
got Warrior too.
Black Prince was never seen, 'presumed lost'.
Or maybe 'still circling the world'.
(My father quoted the sick joke).

'Three down', he said.
'Not that powder-monkeys like me
knew more than cordite dust;
bolted below deck,
cased in thirteen thousand tons.'

HMS Duke of Edinburgh: fourth in line.
Percival, the Captain, bloodshot
with rage and fear, piped ninety degrees west;
fled at nine knots
with one whole ship,
grey virgin of battle,
and eight hundred men, saved.
Headed home for the first of June,
… but in disgrace in some eyes.
'That's about all there was to it', said Dad.
'Mind, I had seven and sixpence bounty
for being there.'

My father could make things –
sheds, walls. Make things go –
crackle-whisker wireless sets,
mowers and kites and hoops.
Play the fife, mouth-organ, concertina.
Grew fine beans and tomatoes.
Swung a parabolic axe
and threw a nifty dart.
Did things in chapel and village. Spun yarns about the old days.
Kept his medals in a box. Lost now.
Brought me into history.

Mike Barlow

The Candles

'They do not want to hold themselves together'.
Kim Moore, 'Candles'

They are tired of being metaphors: remembrances,
prayers. They are tired of the gloom of old churches
where the draught from the aisle is not the breath of angels.
They are tired of power cuts, tents, intimate soirées.

They are tallow and wick. They burn, are consumed,
their last act of falling is pooled wax,
sooty skin cooling, a charred stub of string.

Yes, let us say there was a flame once. It went out.
There will be others. They too will go out.
Our hearts also are tired, our souls dark, but we –
we are the candle-lighters, wedded to metaphor.

Robert Spencer

Summer 1914

It seemed as if
all time, all hope, all humanity
was buffered in that summer,
the old world, deference
and indifference together
in suspension under
a high sun, waiting, waiting,
for a path from catastrophe,
a path to a new world

It seemed as if
they knew, the labourers,
the factory workers, the shop keepers
the farm hands, the office clerks,
the wives, the lovers, the mothers
baking bread, all pretending
it was just another summer
but somehow knowing
it was no such thing

It seemed as if
the deer had slipped away,
bounding over the rough grass,
effortlessly over a layered hedge;
it appeared to drop
before the shot blasted out,
such is the gap between sight and sound.
A thousand miles away another shot
ended another life and another summer

It seemed as if
they had pre-penned their titles,
Strange Meeting,
Dulce Et Decorum Est,
ready for words
to slide into verses
just as the remains of men
would slide into the pools and trenches
so soon to scour a stricken land,
like lashes across a tethered back.

It seemed as if
there would never be enough corners
in those foreign fields.

Anna Johnson

The Artist at the Front: David Jones's *In Parenthesis*

David Jones (1895-1974) was an artist and poet whose work had a profound effect on many of his contemporaries: Eliot, Auden, Bunting and MacDiarmid praised his writing. Eliot (his editor and friend) was a particular champion, stating that: 'The work of David Jones has some affinity with that of James Joyce... and with the later work of Ezra Pound, and with my own'.[1] Auden wrote sensitive, deeply enthusiastic reviews of both of Jones's published long poems, *In Parenthesis* (1937) and *The Anathemata* (1952), and wrote to tell him, 'your work makes me feel very small and madly jealous'.[2] Later poets would cite him as an influence; amongst them Geoffrey Hill and Seamus Heaney. Despite these accolades, he still holds a precarious position in the canon.[3]

As I write this, Jones's two long poems *In Parenthesis* and *The Anathemata* are back in print after a hiatus, the body of criticism is growing steadily, and a three day international conference on his work took place in Oxford in September 2014.[4] It is particularly fitting that an article on Jones be included in this special 'War' edition of *Agenda*. The journal bears his wonderful, idiosyncratic inscription. It was a publication close to his heart, and published a special edition on his writing in 1974.[5] All of Jones's writing and much of his painting reflects his experience of the First World War, and it was the memory of the War which prompted Jones to 'try to make a shape in words' for the first time, moving from visual art to poetry. He began to write his first long poem, *In Parenthesis,* in 1928, nine years after his own demobilization. There are few truly visual poems about the First World War, and *In Parenthesis* is a unique and astonishing achievement. It bears all

---

[1] From an updated 'Note of Introduction': David Jones, *In Parenthesis* (London, 1963), pp. vii-viii. This edition is hereafter cited as '*IP*' by page number in the text.

[2] Letter to Jones from Auden, sent care of Harman Grisewood on 23 February 1954, now held at the Archive of the National Library of Wales, folder CT 2/2, p. 15. Grisewood had thanked Auden on Jones's behalf for his review of Jones's *The Anathemata,* published in *Encounter* in 1954.

[3] See Elizabeth Judges, 'Notes on the Outside: David Jones, "Unshared Backgrounds," and (The Absence of) Canonicity', *Essays in Literary History,* LXVIII, i, (Baltimore, Spring 2001), p. 181.

[4] This conference 'David Jones: Christian Modernist?' took place from 10-13 September 2014, at St Anne's College and Regent's Park College Oxford. It was convened by Professor Paul Fiddes, Dr Erik Tonning, and Dr Anna Johnson.

[5] Vol. 11 No. 4-Vol. 12 No.1 (2 issues) Autumn-Winter 1973/4. This edition contained the unfinished draft of Jones's *The Kensington Mass.* The publishing imprint 'Agenda Editions' went on to print further of his unpublished works and letters through the 1970s and into the 1980s.

the hallmarks of Jones's apprenticeship as an artist, and it is technically innovative and clearly modernist in ways that would not have been possible had it been written during the War.

The influences at work within *In Parenthesis* immediately point to the hybrid nature of Jones's thought as a writer and a painter. The frontispiece illustration to the poem (reproduced as the front cover for this edition of *Agenda*) shows a wounded soldier, alone in the moonlight, caught on the wire of No-Man's Land, arms akimbo and near-cruciform. This soldier is literally entangled in the ferocious inhuman bustle of trench warfare; his flesh is torn and stripped naked. He is a modern version of Blake's 'Albion', and a counterpart of Orpen's 'Blown Up'.[6] It took Jones many drafts to reach the final form of his poem, and in the last part of this essay I will explore some aspects of the poem's shaping, which again bears the imprint of his training as an artist. All the drafts possess the confidence of a far more experienced writer, and Jones's revisions show a deft grasp of modernist poetics. They are imbued with an art-historical knowledge and facility for 'art citation' which make his poetry particularly unusual. Of the First World War poets, only Rosenberg shares Jones's visual articulacy. A year after the publication of *In Parenthesis*, in 1938, Jones wrote to his friend Harman Grisewood: 'I absolutely and definitely know there is *nothing* else I care about except this drawing business – *writing*, ah yes – *as much* – but after all, my equipment is that of a painter not a writer.[7]

Jones was born and grew up in Rotherhithe in London, with Welsh ancestry on his father's side. His early art training at Camberwell School of Art had just ended when Jones signed up to fight in January 1915, joining the ranks of the 15th London Welsh Battalion of the Royal Welch Fusiliers (he had originally wished to join the Artist's Rifles, but that was not to be). He had been eager to enlist, and yet when he came to write his 1937 'War Book' *In Parenthesis*, he portrayed the conflict in its Preface as an interruption of ordinary lives: 'for us amateur soldiers [...] and especially for the writer [...] the war itself was a parenthesis. How glad we were to step outside its brackets at the end of '18' [*IP*, 'Preface', xv].

After his demobilization in 1919, in the calm of peacetime Jones's visual aesthetic matured, first during his time at Westminster College of Art where he was introduced to British Post-Impressionist theory. The second major period of his artistic development took place between 1922 and 1926, when he lived for long periods of time alongside the community of the artist and

[6] See Jonathan Miles and Derek Shiel, *David Jones: The Maker Unmade (Bridgend, 2003)*, p. 213.
[7] Letter from David Jones to Harman J Grisewood, 14 February 1938 in René Hague ed., *Dai Greatcoat: A Self-Portrait of David Jones in his Letters* (London, 1980), p. 83.

sculptor Eric Gill, first at Ditchling Common, and later at Capel-y-ffin in the Black Mountains of Wales. Here, he embraced his new Catholic faith, and grew acquainted with the neo-scholastic thought of Jacques Maritain. He was particularly compelled by Maritain's writings on aesthetics, which embraced Post-Impressionist art theory. It was a time of formal artistic experiment, in which Jones began to develop his ideas of the centrality of art to a humane society, and his idea of man as the only 'gratuitous maker'. These are central themes of all his writings, and Jones would carry on the work of Ruskin, and (to a degree) the views of his own mentor Gill in polarising the defining quality of man's human, 'sign-making' impulse, against the banality of machine-made products. All of this newly acquired knowledge from the 1920s would shape *In Parenthesis*.

Jones's first contribution to the artistic community that he had joined at Ditchling was an engraving which he entitled 'Westward, Ho!'. This [Fig. 1] depicts a soldier on the march, bowed down wearily under his rifle and pack. Eric Gill carved a replica of this image onto the Trumpington War Memorial near Cambridge in 1922, and so Jones's first public attempt to give an artistic representation of the war in which he served was in the form of conventional (if unusually 'realistic') monumental commemoration.[8] The sheer number of war grave commissions taken on by Gill at this time must have underscored Jones's sense of loss. *In Parenthesis* opens with an inscription page that is visually self-conscious about the practice of making a memorial. As Jon Stallworthy notes, 'Printed in capital letters and without punctuation, it looks like a war memorial and sounds like a poem':[9]

> THIS WRITING IS FOR MY FRIENDS
> IN MIND OF ALL COMMON & HIDDEN
> MEN AND OF THE SECRET PRINCES
> AND TO THE MEMORY OF THOSE
> WITH ME IN THE COVERT AND IN
> THE OPEN (...)
> (...) AND TO THE ENEMY
> FRONT-FIGHTERS WHO SHARED OUR
> PAINS AGAINST WHOM WE FOUND
> OURSELVES BY MISADVENTURE

---

[8] See Judith Collins, *Eric Gill, the Sculpture, a Catalogue Raisonné* (London, 1988), p. 43. She notes that 'Gill was not afraid to include realistic modern details in his memorials, such as the gun and the tin hat'. She notes that the most typical attitude of soldiers carved on war memorials was 'upright and alert'.

[9] Jon Stallworthy *Survivors' Songs: From Maldon to the Somme*, Cambridge University Press (Cambridge, 2008) pp. 24-25

Fig 1. David Jones 'Westward Ho!' (1921) Wood engraving. Private Collection.
Image from Miles and Shiel, *David Jones: The Maker Unmade* (Brigend 2003).

The poem announces itself as an elegy and a memorial to all the dead, and also more narrowly, to a particular 'company' of men in a specific time and a place. 'I have only tried', Jones wrote in the Preface, 'to make a shape in words, using as data the complex of sights, sounds, fears, hopes, apprehensions, things exterior and interior, the landscape and paraphernalia of that singular time and those particular men' [*IP* 'Preface', x].

The narrative of *In Parenthesis* follows the adventures of 'B Company' through their early training in Britain, their embarkation to France and movement into the trenches, and ends with their attack on German defences at 'Acid Copse' (part of the Battle of the Somme) in July 1916. This episode is based on Jones's own experience of an attack on Mametz Wood, in which many of his Battalion were killed. The poem imagines the final attack vividly and painfully. An infantryman called 'Dai' is badly wounded. Carried by stretcher bearers, the barrage intensifies overhead and the group duck down to the ground. We hear their anxious, rapid and profanity-laced instructions; 'lower you lower you prize Maria Hunt ... down cantcher – low – hands away me ducky'. The verse then pleads and prays, lullaby-like (perhaps these are the thoughts of the bearers, or perhaps of Dai himself), 'curroodle mother earth/ she's kind:/ pray her hide you in her deeps' [*IP*, 176]. There's no answer to the prayer, no hiding from 'this ferocious pursuer', the bomb which falls to meet them:

> There, there, it can't, won't hurt – nothing
> shall harm my beautiful.
>   But on its screaming passage
> their numbers writ
> and stout canvas tatters drop as if they'd salvoed grape to the
> mizzen-sheets and the shaped ash grip rocket-sticks out of
> the evening sky right back by Bright Trench
> and clots and a twisted clout
> on the bowed back of the F.O.O. bent to his instrument
>   [*IP*, 177]

In the face of such a death, a graven memorial provides some cold but lasting comfort. On the one hand, *In Parenthesis* mirrors a real experience and sets out to 'make a memorial'. On the other, it is a fictionalised account based on real events, 'shaped' through a filter of lived experience and artistic development, and littered with references to a lifetime of reading. The elegiac and deliberately monumental form of its opening inscription draws the reader's attention to the idea of physical 'shaping' and concrete artefact which lie at the very heart of Jones's conception of the arts.

In Parenthesis belongs to the sort of belated writing about the First World War which Andrew Rutherford describes as very different to the 'immediate experience' poems of Owen or Sassoon, or Rosenberg; 'The poems [of immediate experience] still stand as memorials to the suffering of a generation and as warnings for the future; but as time went on the poets and other imaginative writers who survived the war seem to have felt increasingly the need to return to their experiences, to recollect them now in tranquillity or to exorcise them in any case more comprehensively and on a larger scale'.[10] The belatedness of Jones's writing meant that he could experiment with form and scale, and he was conscious of this freedom. His 'painterly equipment', meanwhile, would shape both the content and form of his poem profoundly.

The artist at the Front – form and formlessness in mechanised warfare

Jones believed that his war experience was split into two distinct eras, and the narrative of *In Parenthesis* broadly follows this split chronology. The visual aesthetics of the poem also follow the distinctions between these time periods. The first period (December 1915–July 1916) before the battle of the Somme (and traced in Parts One to Four of the poem), was a time where despite hardship, the men who served together were able to forge friendships. They trained together, 'dug in' together, and created a domestic life of sorts.

During the Somme and after, the depersonalisation, mechanisation and 'wholesale slaughter' [*IP*, 'Preface', ix] horrified Jones. His antipathy to the machine (and particularly its role in war) would haunt his writing and painting ever after. *In Parenthesis* is remarkable in that it takes no sides and holds no grudges. It is the machine and its inventors which are the enemy. British and German soldiers are victims. The German women are imagined in the poem, prior to the Somme attack (we don't know through whose eyes), praying the *Salve Regina* to keep their men from harm; 'O Clemens, O pia and /turn out of alignment the English guns amen' [*IP*, 149]. B Company aren't altogether heroic, they are frank in their homesickness, they sing, '*o my,/ I want-er go home/ I want to go over the foam*' [*IP*, 104]. They discuss the vicissitudes of war and try to second-guess the intentions of 'High Command' in an attempt to gain some purchase on the shape of the conflict [*IP*, 112]. The soldiers are forced to make do with charcoal-drawn approximations:

---

[10] Andrew Rutherford, *The Literature of War: Five Studies in Heroic Virtue* (Macmillan, London, 1978) p. 86.

Like so many Alexanders [...]
[...] they use match-ends
to represent
the dispositions of
fosse and countermure.
[*IP*, 78]

Making these rudimentary plans, the soldiers are artists of a sort, and this inference is deliberate. The men of *In Parenthesis* are described as 'makers', artists or artisans of the most fundamental kind. They take pleasure in simple craftsmanship; '[t]hey were almost eager when required to fill sandbags to repair a freshly destroyed defence. They warmed to their work, and found some interest in this remaking' [*IP*, 96]. These are moments of respite, and they give the men leave to imagine themselves in a line of descent: '[t]hey strengthened their hands like the builders at the watergate'. Jones provides a note of explanation: this reference is to Artaxerxes, *Nehemiah* iii and iv, and the rebuilding of Jerusalem's defences.[11] In his mythic, transhistoric 'boast' Dai Greatcoat asserts proudly, 'I built a shit-house for Artaxerxes' [*IP*, 79].

Against the 'unmaking' of war, the soldiers look for wholeness and beauty, taking pleasure in newly-carpentered duckboard planks, 'its joiner-work could, here and there, make quick that delectation of the mind enjoyed with the sight of any common deal, white-pared, newly worked by carpenters' [*IP*, 77]. This 'delectation of the mind' refers to Maritain's description (*pace* Thomas Aquinas) of man's approach to a beautiful object as, '[...] the lightening of intelligence over matter intelligently arranged. The understanding enjoys the beautiful because in it it finds and recognises itself, and gets contact with its own light.'[12] There is no sarcasm, I think, in Jones's decision to give these basic forms such an elevated treatment.

One of the soldiers of *In Parenthesis*, the clumsy Private Ball, has an educated artistic eye. He is something of a parade's disgrace (his pack is 'ill-adjusted and without form' [*IP*, 2]) but he has an artist's way of seeing. He is capable of transforming the early scenes of the war into a painting of the mid-fifteenth century, Paulo Uccello's 'Battle of San Romano': 'From where he stood heavily, irksomely at ease, he could see, half-left between 7 and 8 of the front rank, the profile of Mr. Jenkins and the elegant cut of his war-time rig and his flax head held front; like San Romano's foreground squire, unhelmeted' [*IP*, 2]. Walking in the dark through the trenches tripping over

---

[11] See *IP*, 212, note 46.
[12] Jacques Maritain, *The Philosophy of Art: "Art et Scholastique"*, transl. Rev. John O'Connor (Ditchling, 1923), pp. 35-6.

objects, he remembers his art night-class, and the obstacles become 'wooden donkeys for the shins of nervous newcomer to the crowded nightclass ... in and out the easel forest in and out barging' [*IP*, 32-3]. He has an affinity with Jones's 1915 'self', just out of Camberwell School of Art. But we learn through his eyes that an image from the past cannot be easily superimposed on the shapes of the present; 'we don't have lances now nor banners nor trumpets. It pains the lips to think of bugles – and did they blow Defaulters on the Uccello horns' [*IP*, 2]. Past and present fall apart again, as the Sergeant upbraids Ball for marching 'easy', and he notes that 'The Squire from the Rout of San Romano smokes Melachrino No. 9.' [*IP*, 5]. Reality won't quite conform to Ball's medieval, chivalric ideal.

There is almost never a clear narrating voice in *In Parenthesis*. We see through the eyes of soldiers one after another; we don't always know who is seeing and who is speaking, although we can often guess at this by the way in which they respond. Because of this technical achievement, the poem conveys its central ironies with subtlety. The most obvious irony of the poem lies in the discrepancy between the soldiers' wish to make 'order' and 'form' from their experience (just as the writer later attempts to 'make order' from remembered events), when they don't possess the insight of their commanding officers, and when their artistry is likely to be undone on the instant by the artillery barrage.

It is the earlier, more humane period in the war (behind front lines, in a place of relative safety) which allows the soldiers to respond like artists to visual stimuli. As we progress to the Somme, later sections of the poem make the irony of the men's disenfranchisement more apparent; they are forced to look harder for 'form' in the formlessness. A shell-hole becomes 'an exactly drawn circle' [*IP*, 34], and the moonlight 'transfigures' the wounded landscape, so that it becomes 'filigreed' [*IP*, 35], and later, 'damascened' [*IP*, 98]. But the reader is invited, time and time again, to see behind these 'forms'. If man-made forms can redeem, man-made formlessness is horror, particularly so when it exemplifies man's inhumanity to man. Under the moonlight, the newly drafted B company process along the trenches and see the shapes of 'once-bodies' lifted from the slime. This is one of the most unflinching passages of the poem, and it is intensely moving:

They lift things, and a bundle-thing out; its shapelessness sags. From this muck-raking are singular stenches, long decay leavened; compounding this clay, with that more precious, patient of baptism; chemical-corrupted once-bodies. They've served him barbarously – poor Johnny – you wouldn't desire him, you wouldn't know him for any other.   [*IP*, 43]

Finally, we are told that the men are not the artists of their conflict, but the disenfranchised 'hands' (factory workers). The voice of Eric Gill can be heard very strongly in the following passage (and this is a rare, 'authorial' interjection), condemning the gap of perception which exists between conscripted soldier and the strategists who plan their engagements, 'You know no more than do those hands who squirt cement till siren screams, who are indifferent that they rear an architect's folly; read in the press perhaps the grandeur of the scheme.' [*IP*, 87]

The Genesis of visual tropes in Part Five of *In Parenthesis*

Chapter Five of *In Parenthesis* marks the turning point within the poem from the early more 'humane' era, to the start of the Somme offensive. It is also the most visually sophisticated section of the poem. Through a careful juxtaposition of aesthetics borrowed from the sphere of the visual arts, Jones makes the change apparent. He does this by emulating the visual tactics of an avant-garde British 'machine art', at its height just prior to the outbreak of war in 1914. Jones's models here are likely to have been British Vorticism, and European Futurism. Jones never felt any personal liking for the foremost proponent of machine art in pre-First World War Britain, Percy Wyndham Lewis. This was to some extent the product of later clashes (in the 1950s, Lewis aggressively attacked Jones's mythological paintings as a window on a 'fairy-book world').[13] Despite this later animosity, there was an early connection between the two artists. In his years at Westminster, Jones made careful readings of Hulme's *Speculations*, which preached the tendency towards abstraction and were fundamentally important to Lewis. More importantly, the artist Bernard Meninsky promoted cubist and Vorticist theory, and taught Jones at Westminster School of Art. Tom Dilworth notes:

> By the mid-1920s the formation of [Jones's] mature visual aesthetic reached a plateau. During these years his paintings are fairly realistic, though stylized. Objects and figures securely located in uniform perspective are solid, weighted, and somewhat tubular, with heavily defined and shaded, hard outer edges. These paintings seem indebted to the vorticist influence of Bernard Meninsky, who exhibited with the vorticists and taught Jones at Westminster School

---

[13] See Wyndham Lewis, 'Round the London Art Galleries' in *The Listener*, XXXIX, mxi, 10 June 1948. Lewis writes, 'Mr. David Jones has a number of large and characteristic water-colours representing a fairy-book world', p. 944.

of Art. I remember Jones saying, furthermore, that he admired the work of Wyndham Lewis.[14]

The Vorticist movement was over by 1918, but reflecting on its achievements in 1939, Wyndham Lewis wrote that 'Vorticism accepted the machine-world: that is the point to stress. It sought out machine-forms. The pictures of the Vorticist were a sort of *machines*. This, of course, serves to define Vorticism as the opposite of an 'escapist' doctrine. It was cheerfully and dogmatically external.'[15] Lewis here pits the 'externality' of the machine aesthetic against those who would prefer an intellectual and artistic 'escape' from the brutal reality of a mechanistic world.[16] He argues that far from extolling the virtues of the machine – in a form of propaganda – Vorticism simply took its cue from reality.

There is a great deal of defensive posturing in this address (Lewis entitled it 'The Skeleton in the Cupboard Speaks'). In the inter-war period, Vorticism was entirely out of favour for its pre-War belligerence. The War had also put paid to the movement's short-lived journal *Blast* (1914-15); many of its early contributors had been killed. With the machine aesthetic now out of favour, Lewis had retrospectively to defend Vorticism's love of mechanism against Futurism: 'It did not sentimentalize machines, as did the Italians, (the pictorial fascists who preceded the political fascists). It took them as a matter of course: just as we take trees, hills, rivers, coal deposits [...] it was a stoic creed: it was not an *uplift*.'[17] Moreover, Lewis argues in his own defence, the Vorticists as a British movement knew that their machine aesthetic was 'visual, not functional. That is to say, it did not identify the artist with the machine. The artist *observed* the machine, from the outside.'

This stress on 'observation', not 'identification', points to the particular subject-object dilemmas of both Futurism and Vorticism. When ordering a painting according to the formal exigencies of the machine, how does the artist maintain a critical distance? Lewis persuasively argued for Vorticist 'stillness' and externality against the Italian interest in the 'movement' of machine forms. In so doing, he seems to argue that it was 'animated' depictions of machines that risked too great an identification between artist and machine. These machines in motion look organic, 'like a rose or a

---

[14] See Thomas Dilworth, *The Shape of Meaning in the Poetry of David Jones* (Toronto, 1988), p. 13.
[15] Wyndham Lewis, *Wyndham Lewis the Artist: From Blast to Burlington House* (London, 1939), p. 78.
[16] Here, Lewis is taking Herbert Read to task for his characterization of Vorticism as 'escapist'.
[17] Ibid., p. 79.

sponge'.[18] But as in Futurism, where the pictures of the Vorticists contained human forms, these organic forms become 'a sort of machines'. We think of a work such as David Bomberg's 'In the Hold' (1913-14). Though never really conscripted into the Vorticist movement, identifying in the pre-War period with Futurism, C. R. W. Nevinson's 'La Mitrailleuse' (1915) is another demonstration of how far man and machine could be identified, whilst maintaining a firm foothold in realism. Works such as these, taken together with Lewis's 1939 statement, raise the question of how the Vorticist artist, in making man conform to the geometry of the machine, retains man's humanity, and keeps his own distance as an observer. Does this melding of man and machine signify an 'uplift' of machines, or does it constitute a diminishing of man's humanity?

Jones understood these debates raging around the machine aesthetic in the 1920s, and borrowed from them in his poem, where a troubled identification of man and machine, and opposing 'pictures' of war refuse to reconcile the mechanised present with the past. Going back to the 'San Romano' section of Part Two, we are told that 'John Ball regained a certain quietness and an indifference to what might be, as his loaded body moved forward unchoosingly as part of a mechanism another mile or so'. [IP, 19] Here, Ball is forced to conform to a militarily 'pleasing' visual order which he associates with Paolo Uccello's depictions of battle.[19] His 'mechanisation' is an unwilling one, and we soon see why. As B Company pass down the communication trenches, they gaze in fear at sidings where 'a rigid medley thrown about – iron and wood and iron, made evidently to some precise requirement, shaped to some usage yet unknown to any of that halting company; who looked on wonderingly, with half inquisitive, half fearful, glancing' [IP, 19-20]. These are men who don't yet understand the kind of war they are in, but have begun to fear its props.

As we progress through the poem, the mechanisation of the men becomes more complex. Silhouetted against the sky, Sgt. Ryan is an enigma to his men:

You suppose the texture of his soul to inform the dark and exact contour his buff coating describes against the convulsed cones of light; he would seem of one piece with his slanted iron hat-rim – he who is an amiable cuckold – yet how should we his True Love

---

[18] Ibid.
[19] Modernist artists such as Lewis borrowed Uccello's high perspective when making paintings of trench warfare: such a view was necessary for capturing the subterranean trench life of the conflict. See Richard Cork, *A Bitter Truth: Avant-Garde Art and the Great War* (London, 1994), p. 9. Cork notes that the exigencies of depicting trench warfare forced Modernist artists to underpin 'their war images with precedents from the distant past'.

know, we on whom he turns his rigid heel, at whom he barks, to
bloody well fall-in – Jump on these fag ends!

[*IP*, 109]

The observer here identifies him as inextricably of one piece with his
military clothing. Here we have Jones's typical leap from formal, visual
language – 'the dark and exact contour [...] the convulsed cones of light'
– to literary allusion: 'Yet how should we his True Love know'. Echoing
Ophelia's mad song, this interjection underscores a central truth about
Sgt. Ryan's presentation. He can be viewed as a man-mechanism (the
poem implies) only because he is not well known, and not well-liked. The
men only know him by hearsay and superficial reputation; he is a harsh
disciplinarian. Faced with his belligerence, the soldiers' imaginations have
little to go on.

When an abstracting machine aesthetic is 'translated' from the visual art
into literature, its distortions are conveyed through literary metaphor. As
Sol Worth has argued when considering the similarities of verbal metaphor
and visual caricature, metaphor can be viewed as a 'metastructure dealing
with a code which is transformed upon a variety of modes'. These modes
can include the visual and the verbal. As Worth suggests, in both literary
and visual art, metaphor (appearing in art as visual abstraction) relies
upon the recognition both of similarity and of difference. [20] So through *In
Parenthesis*, we see man as 'part' of a mechanism, seeming to merge with it
and to adopt its geometric lines and planes; then we learn that the metaphor
will not hold (Ball moves 'unchoosingly', Sgt. Ryan is unknowable). In
this way, the poem expresses the obvious limitations of the machine as a
means of ordering reality.

Part Five of the poem contains a neat, visual depiction of men on the
march so brilliantly ordered and geometric in its presentation as to give
pause for thought, if we have assumed (from the examples given so far)
that Jones's treatment of man as machine always contains its own internal
critique:

In three quarters of an hour they passed, making the shutters rattle.
She could see their efficient looking iron hats, between where the
taped curtains nearly met at the middle pane; in fourfold recession,
subtly elliptical, each one tilted variously yet in a strict alignment,
like pegs on a rigid string. Words of command lost shape against the

---

[20] See Sol Worth, 'Seeing Metaphor as Caricature, *New Literary History*, VI, xi (1974) 195-209,
p. 199.

Above left. Fig 2.a, Luigi Russolo, 'La Rivolta' (1911), Oil on canvas, Collection Gemeentemuseum Den Haag, The Hague.
Above right, Fig 2.b, Christopher Richard Wynne Nevinson 'Returning to the Trenches' (1914-1915). Oil on canvas. National Gallery of Canada, Ottawa.

> sealed windows; the beam of light from her oil lamp shone on them
> through the glass, shined on cleaned numerals, and on the piling-
> swivels of rifles slung.
>
> [*IP*, 104-105]

The efficient-looking hats make similarly efficient visual patterns. They are not tilted to the same angle (this would be unrealistic), but they maintain their 'strict alignment' which shows that the men, marching four deep, are perfectly in line. The 'piling-swivels of rifles' (metal gadgets affixed to the nose of rifles, which would allow them to be stacked together), and the 'numerals' (probably brass regimental shoulder titles) are caught in the beam of the lamp. All this military gear, we can assume, maintains the orderly 'recession', and it is the recession of forms which would give us a sense of perspective if this were a visual image.

Jones's depiction of successive rows of men caught in beams of light, in recession, is comparable to the techniques of some Futurist paintings, for example, Luigi Russolo's 'La Rivolta' [Fig 2.a]. Nevinson's 'Returning to the Trenches' [Fig 2.b] exploits similar tactics; the French soldiers are treated in typically mechanised terms. Their bodies are geometric, and a fast forward movement is suggested by the aggressive diagonals of their forward-leaning bodies. Jones's manuscript drafts for this section show that his image of these men marching had emerged, almost fully realised in the earliest stages of the compositional process:

> In three-quarters of an hour they passed
> making the shutters ~~very slightly~~ rattle.
> She could see their efficient looking iron hats

between where the taped curtains nearly met
across the ~~lower~~ upper door-pane.
in four-fold recession, subtly elliptical,
each one titled variously, yet in strict alignment
as if slung on a rigid string.
words of command ~~beat inarticulate against the~~
Broke ~~muted~~ against the sealed windows[21]

This passage would undergo a number of revisions (the image of successive waves of helmets and guns caught in a beam of light, reminiscent of Futurist 'force-lines', is not yet developed). Insofar as it mimics the efficiencies of the machines themselves, it exemplifies the tactics of Futurism; the one jarring note is the description of helmets, 'slung on a rigid string', becoming in the final version like 'pegs on a rigid string', a domestic image of washing pegged out on the line. In an earlier draft Jones writes 'as/ if slung on a taut bar'[22], so this inclusion of a homely conceit was deliberate.[23] But this in itself is not enough to destabilize the impact of these soldiers as part of a mechanism, viewed through the filter of an efficient, geometricizing aesthetic. For that, we need a subjective voice to reflect on the disorderly, incidental and human aspects of the scene.

It is here that we meet the viewer, Alice. She runs a small café, a 'mean estaminet' just behind the lines. The café has been swallowed up by the encircling conflict, and the British soldiers of B Company go there in their time-off, drink the 'abominable beer' [*IP*, 112], and dream of home. She is on the inside of the window-pane looking out (the 'Looking Glass' comparison is intentional), as the battalion of men move up the line. In the finished version of *In Parenthesis*, Alice is represented *after* the 'objective' block of text describing the marching, efficient soldiers, in a separate block of text, making the division visually apparent:

She counted to herself, her rounded elbows lifted, as Boucher liked them, held within the action – she put down the glass, half-wiped: forty-four sections of four across the ray, not counting odd bobbing ones and twos who hurry after – that was more than last time; she had wondered for these newer ones, in their ill-filled-out tunics,

[21] National Library of Wales Archive, 'David Jones Papers', Folder LP 1/6, *In Parenthesis*: early manuscript drafts, 1927-1933', title 'Part V 1927-1933', f. 11 (library numbering).
[22] Ibid. f. 10 (library numbering).
[23] C.f., *IP*, 175. In Part Seven, dead soldiers' faces in the moonlight are compared to 'china saucers tilted'.

who crowded with the others and drank *citron*, who were silent as
she passed between the tables, who would dangle their bonnets.

[*IP*, 105]

This passage, juxtaposed with the earlier section, modifies it drastically.
The word 'bonnets' for helmets is clearly Alice's; a pastoral incursion. Alice
notes the 'ill-filled-out tunics'; later, as the men march they discuss the way
to deal with badly-fitting kit; 'if you're a Skinny Lizzie, it's best to put a
sock under the shoulder-straps' [*IP*, 118]. The idiom is motherly and kind,
and Alice notices that the raw new recruits are awkward and speechless.
She is visually perceptive, counting 'forty-four sections of four across the
ray'. Her 'odd bobbing ones following after' destroys the rigid symmetry
of the first passage – a similar effect, in fact, to the somewhat disordered
presentation of Nevinson's returning French soldiers. Despite the strong
horizontals, Nevinson's soldiers do not quite hold the line, and strange objects
in the foreground (perhaps mess-tins and packs) disrupt the symmetry. These
jarring features give a sense of disorder, and panicked retreat.

Alice, as observer, is also observed in the passage above. What is most
interesting, when this is compared with Jones's early manuscript drafts,
is how little of her interior thought is left. Initially, her 'section' is much
longer and more discursive, and comes before the 'men seen through the
window' section:

The beam of light from her oil-lamp shone on
them through the glass.
Shone on their battle-gear.
She remembered, according to Jacques, her great-grandfather
had helped to kill a Marquis with a scythe
after Valmy
[...] Perhaps she knew her great grand father had marched in the
 rain to
the mill at Valmy
Anyhow she nearly sang the Marseillaise.
She counted to herself in the French tongue,
her plump elbows raised, ~~attractively~~ as Boucher rather liked them,
held
within the action: she put down the glass half wiped.[24]

The manuscript drafts show that Jones made many more attempts

[24] Wales, National Library, folder LP1/6, f. 24 (library numbering)

to include this family history for Alice.[25] Another draft records how her grandfather 'wretchedly fumbled with damp gun cotton'.[26] But Jones finally crosses out the 'grandfather' lines. He then makes a breakthrough, separating the 'soldiers' side of the scene from the 'Alice' side, placing them first, and her second.

I believe that the cutting-down of the 'Alice' passage came as a result of Jones's realisation that the marching figures as a visual device could be best contrasted with Alice if she was predominantly viewed as a visual emblem herself. She becomes one of the feminine figures in a Boucher painting. As Jo Hedley notes:

> The art of François Boucher is instantly recognisable: its rococo palette, luscious female nudes and be-ribboned pastorals have been both praised and dismissed as light, sensual and elitist. For some it is the visual archetype of decadent *ancien régime* frivolity, thankfully swept away by David and the French Revolution. Others, nostalgic for a lost era of aristocratic elegance untrammelled by utilitarian concerns, see Boucher's work as the embodiment of a "moment of perfection in French Art', conceived in essentially decorative terms.[27]

It is this 'be-ribboned' pastoral aspect of Boucher's work that Jones was initially trying to capture. Early drafts begin with Alice fastening a scarf or bonnet: 'she ~~looked~~ glanced down to arrange again some ~~strayed~~ loosened flimsiness, puckering ~~a pleasing~~/ a fullness about her chin/ she finger tipped her drawn back hair'.[28] Jones's love of Boucher's mannerisms, the hands 'held within the action' is evident in many of his own pencil sketches which depict female figures in the middle of an 'action', particularly holding flowers.[29]

As the drafts progress, Alice's patriotism and personal history are subsumed beneath the visual 'emblem' of this non-specific reference to Boucher. This is a fascinating indicator of how the 'inscape' (to borrow from Hopkins – Jones used this word often) of a character might be replaced by a visual idea to express the characteristics of a time and a place. In this case, the

[25] Ibid., f. 24. Further references to her Grandfather at Valmy are crossed out at f. 27, and thereafter disappear.

[26] Ibid., f. 26.

[27] See Ex. Cat., Jo Hedley, *Françoise Boucher: Seductive Visions*, Wallace Collection, to accompany the exhibition *Boucher: Seductive Visions* held at the Wallace Collection, London, 30 September 2004 to 17 April 2005 (London, 2004), p. 13.

[28] Wales, National Library, folder LP1/6, f. 11.

[29] See Nicolete Gray, *The Paintings of David Jones* (London, 1989), cat. 58. 'Escaping Figure Carrying Trinkets' (late 1930s) and cat. 59. 'Girl Holding Flowers' (1939). See also See Miles and Shiel, 'Portraits and Friends' in *The Maker Unmade*, pp. 150-164.

time and place represented by Boucher is pre-Revolutionary France. When we lose Alice's thoughts of singing the Marseillaise and her recollections of a grandfather at Valmy, we also lose sight of France's troubled political history, and Alice and her husband Jacques become entirely representative of a comic pastoral scene. Their estaminet becomes an emblem or outpost of a peacetime world.

Jones decides to make a conscious break between past and present here, for the sake of greater contrast between Alice's world, and the soldiers'. In the final version, she has no historic remembrance of war to draw on, but Jones retains her compassion, which shapes how the reader sees these 'mechanised' men.[30] She 'wonders for' the new recruits, notices with foreboding the increase in numbers. The technical discovery which Jones makes in his drafts for this section of Part Five is the separation of the two blocks of text; their opposing points of view and opposing aesthetics represent the window, or rather, the views from either side of it. The text becomes a two-way mirror or looking glass, presenting two images of war and peacetime that gaze in confusion across the divide. Past and present will not cohere; pastoral and machine aesthetic face one another, and Alice tells us how to 'read' the image of mechanised efficiency, and also to see through it.

Writing much later on the eve of another war, Jones described the continuity of experience between the men at Crécy and the modern day soldiers (both contending with the appalling French mud). He writes that the 'Bombarde' of that earlier conflict 'presaged the "scream of the twelve-inch shrapnel"', and the coming world of material-as-power'.[31] He was always interested in the line of descent from past wars to present, but one of his most radical achievements in *In Parenthesis* is an imaginative and visual depiction of the impasse between then, and now. In the Preface to the poem, he writes; '[w]e feel a rubicon has been passed between striking with a hand weapon as men used to do and loosing poison from the sky as we do ourselves. We doubt the decency of our own inventions, and are certainly in terror of their possibilities.' [*IP*, 'Preface', xiv]

The 'humane' artistry of the soldiers of *In Parenthesis,* set against the riving power of ballistics and polarised throughout the poem, is now seen as a central concern of Modernist writing. Douglas Mao, in his recent work *Solid Objects: Modernism and the Test of Production* describes the

---

[30] There is also (in the final version) a faint animosity towards Alice and Jacques as war profiteers, symbols of a rural age but also possessed of a mercenary cunning: 'She said that the war was lucrative, and chid him feed the fowl, and smoothed her apron' [*IP*, 106].
[31] Ibid., p. 128.

modernist 'encounter with the object' as being frequently one of 'horror' at the otherness of things, their 'non-human Being'.[32] But this existentialist dilemma is mediated by the love of the crafted object, for 'although few if any modernists were immune to the pleasures of consumption, most also showed a profound mistrust of the capitalist formations that made what Adorno called a 'culture industry' possible, and virtually all promoted the carefully crafted work of art as an alternative to the fruits of mass production and mass marketing'.[33]

Jones is remarkable for turning this 'encounter with the object' into an encounter with (and critique of) modern warfare, subtly holding up to the light those objects which had lost all connection to human beings. War is the most obvious culmination of a mass-producing, stockpiling mentality. Warmongers within *In Parenthesis* such as the 'mild young' Bombing Officer who appears in Part One of the poem, see only the efficiency of war (the power and 'efficiency' of its ballistics), not its cost. The men in the trenches are forced into the position of factory 'hands', and can only guess at the shape of the machine that they build. They are the technics in the scheme, and the inventions of this war are the opposite of love, the opposite of compassion.

The defining message of *In Parenthesis* is one of essential humanity, in which artistic 'making' is seen as an intrinsic human quality. The compassion which the soldiers of *In Parenthesis* have for one another (and also for their enemy) is contrasted sharply with the degradations of mechanical warfare. The soldiers of the poem will not conform to the shapes of the machines, and they are continually on the look-out for beauty, for form, for marks of the human. As Jones writes much later in a poem entitled 'A, a, a, Domine Deus' (he called this his 'signature tune', and it appeared in the 1974 *Agenda* Special Edition), it is the condition of modern man to look, even in the 'unfamiliar' shapes of mechanically produced objects and architecture, to seek the evidence of man, and the presence of God:

> I have looked for a long while
> at the textures and contours.
> I have run a hand over the trivial intersections.
> I have journeyed among the dead forms
> causation projects from pillar to pylon.

---

[32] Douglas Mao, *Solid Objects: Modernism and the Test of Production*, (Princeton, New Jersey, 1998), p. 17. He identifies the subject/object dilemmas of Virginia Woolf as a form of existentialist 'nausea' – the thinking, feeling subject confronting 'the discrete object, as the particular representative or crystallization of non-human Being'.

[33] Ibid., p. 18.

I have tired the eyes of the mind
           Regarding the colours and lights.
I have felt for His Wounds
    in nozzles and containers.
I have wondered for the automatic devices.
I have tested the inane patterns
    without prejudice.
I have been on my guard
    not to condemn the unfamiliar.
For it is easy to miss Him
    at the turn of a civilisation.[34]

---

[34] David Jones, *The Sleeping Lord and other fragments*, (London, 1974), p. 9.

Peter Treherne, 22, Chosen Young Essayist

The Wood of *In Parenthesis*

The critic Paul Fussell considers David Jones's Great War poem *In Parenthesis* to be a conservative work that glorifies rather than laments the war and the soldiers that suffered during it.[1] He goes on to attribute this glorification to the many religious and medieval motifs that have been worked into the body of the poem, and yet he acknowledges that often this ennobling effect misfires, producing instead a great deal of sympathy and real acknowledgment of the suffering of each soldier.

Jones makes an effort to equate these men disembowelled or torn apart by machine guns with dismembered antique gods in sacred groves [...] but now the poem doesn't work the way he wants it to, and we focus only on innocent young Lieutenant Jenkins, who is shot almost immediately, and on Sergeant Quilter, who gets it next, and on 'the severed head of '72 Morgan' (180). [2]

Though Fussell states that the poem *unintentionally* shifts from the apotheosis of the soldier to their human pain I would assert that this is a deliberate technique employed by David Jones to emphasise that suffering.

This theme of suffering is of great personal importance to David Jones. The Great War continued to affect him long after the fighting ended, determining many aspects of his life. 'I always work from a window of a house if it is at all possible. I like looking out on to the world from a reasonably sheltered position': the position of a dug out or a trench.[3] *In Parenthesis*, regardless of its mythical allusions, remains a highly biographical work. The poem describes in seven parts the movement of a group of soldiers, and specifically Private John Ball, from their basic training camp in England, across the Channel, to the Western Front in France. A series of glimpses into the habits and customs of the soldier leads to the poem's climax and conclusion when John Ball and his platoon attack the German positions within a wood and suffer extreme casualties; John Ball himself receives a wound to his leg. Ball's action in the unnamed forest mirrors Jones's own role in the Somme

---

[1] He writes that the 'effect of the poem, for all its horrors, is to rationalise and even to validate the war by implying that it somehow recovers many of the motifs and values of medieval chivalric romance', *The Great War and Modern Memory* (New York: Oxford University Press, 2013), p. 158.

[2] *Ibid.*, p. 164.

[3] From David Blamires, *David Jones: Artist and Writer* (Toronto: University of California Press, 1972), p. 59.

Offensive where he received a wound assaulting German positions in the wood of Mametz. The imagery of the forest as a site of turmoil and struggle appears as a personal and significant trope within Jones's oeuvre, and arguably the afterlife of these images, in *The Anathemata* and *The Sleeping Lord*, reveals the enduring trauma of the Great War for David Jones.

Using the forest or wood of Part 7 of *In Parenthesis* as an example I will explore how the mythical and religious imagery – the imagery of gothic church, of pagan fertility ritual, and of Christ's sacrifice upon the Cross – lends a prevailing mood of affliction and destruction and, in juxtaposition to the mythical allusions, a real and tangible human suffering. The forest as a space where the mythical traditions and religious observances are tied to the suffering of the soldier gives epic proportion to their ordeal, but unlike the allusions, the soldiers' sacrifice is hollow, either remaining unfulfilling or perverted, and so their suffering becomes commensurately more tragic by its misguided and hopeless nature. Hope alone remains in the form of the crucifix and Christ's sacrifice, but it is as beneficiary and not as author that these soldiers receive it.

Turning first to the forest-as-church image, when Private Ball stumbles into the 'vacuum' and 'ancient stillnesses' of the wood in Part 7 he discovers a religious space carved out of the chaos of war.[4]

> Down in the under-croft, in the crypt of the wood, clammy
> drippings percolate – and wide-girth boled the eccentric co-
> lonnade, as perilous altar-house for a White Tower, and a
> cushy place to stuff and garnish and bid him keep him – or
> any nosy-bloody-Parker who would pry on the mysteries.
> Aisle-ways bunged-up between these columns rising,
> these long strangers,
> under this vaulting stare upward,
> for recumbent princes of his people.
> Stone lords coiffed
> long-skirted field-grey to straight fold
> for a coat-armour
> and for a cere-cloth, for men of renown:
> Hardrada-corpse for Froggy sepulture.
>
> (IP 182)

---

4 David Jones, *In Parenthesis* (London: Faber & Faber, 2010), p. 181. All future references to *In Parenthesis* (abbreviated to *IP*) will be cited by page number in text.

The architectural terms of 'colonnade', 'croft', 'vaulting', 'crypt', 'altar' and '[a]isle' merge cathedral and wood, turning the corpses littered there into stone memorials of 'field-grey' knights. The metaphor is not one of medieval fantasy however. These 'recumbent princes', and the vaulting of their church, establishes on a parallel plane to the physical trauma of conflict the idea of desecration. John Ball and his fellow soldiers are the 'nosy-bloody-Parker[s]' that pry upon the sacral stillness of the forest-that-is-church; they have become loathsome Mordreds besieging Queen Guinevere in her White Tower, committing not only sacrilege but attempted regicide.[5] The allusion is thus of civil war and ignoble assault, and this, connected with 'clammy drippings' and the 'bunged-up' aisles, speaks not of an ordered resting place but of a war-swept building, and one that holds already a history of conquest. 'The Hardrada-corpse' elides the conquering Harald of 1066 with the German soldiers of the First World War, who themselves are conquerors, buried in their foreign 'Froggy sepulture'. And beside these giants are to be found, 'death-halsed' (*IP* 182) together, 'a Picton-five-feet-four paragon for the Line' (*IP* 182), the next conqueror to desecrate the forest church.[6] The forest church therefore highlights the destructive nature of war by lending an added moral dubiety to the successive waves of soldiers; their war is not one of religious right but one of sacrilege, and though they may lie like knights in memorial, they commit an act no knight of Christendom should.

In David Jones's 'The Dream of Private Clitus' – a 'fragment' from his collection *The Sleeping Lord* – another forest-church appears.

And looking up at those gusty vaults of the faded green of a
dying year, with chinks of a now darkening blue, flecked from
Westward with the caelian purple – for 'twas near toward the
evening bugle – the mingle of their contesting boughs seemed to
make pointed arches.

Now that's a thing you don't see in stone, Oenomaus, a pointed
arch. And I don't suppose you ever will.

---

[5] The White Tower refers to The Tower of London and Mordred's siege of Lady Guinevere who 'stuffed it [the Tower of London] with all manner of victual, and well garnished it with men': Malory, *Le Morte d'Arthur,* ed. John Mathews (London: Cassell, 2000), II, XXI, I, p 871.

[6] David Jones is playing with the juxtaposition between the diminutive Welshmen and the tall Germans who require, as Hardrada did, 'seven feet of English soil or so much more as he is taller than other men': Snorri Sturluson, *Heimskringla*, trans. Lee M. Hollander (Austin: University of Texas Press, 2002), p. 653.

But it's a fine thing is a pointed arch made of the striving branches
of the living wood.[7]

Importantly, the boughs of this forest cathedral are restless. Mirroring the
'rear-guard' (*SL* 16) conflict that is happening within the wood, the trees'
outspread limbs are 'contesting' and 'striving', or earlier, 'all is thrusting
and directional in the labyrinth of those parts and each swaying limb of each
tree struggles for the mastery, high up' (*SL* 16). A similar passage can be
found in *In Parenthesis*:

> The trees are very high in the wan signal-beam, for whose slow
> gyration their wounded boughs seem as malignant limbs,
> manoeuvring for advantage.
> The trees of the wood beware each other [...]
>
> (*IP* 184)

The church of the forest is not a peaceful place. The 'malignant' trees are
a reference to Beult Wood where Llywelyn, the last king of Wales, met his
death in 1282: and above him, wrote a contemporary, 'the trees of the forest
furiously rush against each other'[8]. According to Jones Llywelyn was found
'decapitated, his head crowned with ivy' and 'a relic of the Cross' (*IP* 211n)
discovered on his person. As such he becomes a Christ figure, enacting the
terrible suffering and sacrifice of the mass, but not within the confines of
a church, but out in the open forest. The same contesting boughs occur in
The Anathemata also, though they are now wearied: 'the genii of spine and
triforium / like great rivals met when all is done, nod recognition across / the
cramped repeats of their dead selves'.[9] The pillars are no longer 'in the sap-
years: / between the living floriations / under the leaping arches' (*Ana* 49) but
have become fossilised reminders of a once hotly contested existence. The
initial 'stillnesses' of the forest church are no longer as the natural order of
things, the quiet of a church or the peacefulness of a tree, is disrupted.
The boughs of the forest church undergo another transformation when

---

[7] David Jones, *The Sleeping Lord* (London: Faber & Faber, 1995), pp. 16-17. All future references
to *The Sleeping Lord* (abbreviated to *SL*) will be cited by page number in text.

[8] *IP*, note 42, pp. 211-12: 'Our last ruler', the last Llywelyn. Killed on December 10th-11th, 1282
near Cefn-y-Bedd in the woods of Beult; decapitated, his head crowned with ivy. A relic of the
Cross was found 'in his breeches pocket'. [...] His contemporary, Gruffyddap yr Ynad Côch, sang
of his death: 'The voice of Lamentation is heard in every place... the course of nature is changed...
the trees of the forest furiously rush against each other.''

[9] David Jones, *The Anathemata* (London: Faber & Faber, 2010), p. 49. All future references to *The
Anathemata* (abbreviated to *Ana*) will be cited by page number in text.

Private Clitus, in a grammatical parallelism, equates 'the trees of those woods' (*SL* 16) with 'the gods of those woods' (*SL* 16). The trees are not just pillars of a single church but individual 'numen' (*SL* 16) or 'failing numina' (*Ana* 49) whose clashing limbs struggle for existence. Biez Wood's foreshadowing of Mametz in Part 4 is a striking example of this religious struggle. John Ball has turned his eyes 'to where the wood thinned to separate broken trees' (*IP* 67) and as he does so he hears the raised song of a German accordion playing '*Es ist ein' Ros' entsprungen / Aus einer Wurzel zart*' (*IP* 67). A war of songs and of cultures emerges as the British try and drown out the German Carol with an aggressive rendition of *Casey Jones*, but complementing this current cultural war is an historical one. Appended to the German Christmas Carol is the following sentence: 'Since Boniface once walked in Odin's wood' (*IP* 67). St Boniface, an Anglo-Saxon from England, lead a missionary expedition to Germany where, as myth states, he cut down a great tree that the pagans worshipped. Religious conflict is thus merged into the make up of the forest. When the British soldiers arrive in the wood they come as 'Jack o' the Green' (*IP* 168) or 'Diana's Jack' (*IP* 66) in an escalating confusion of sacrificial practice. Here 'the tree-spirit Diana, goddess of nature and of fertility' becomes interwoven with 'a northern counterpart to the midsummer sacrifice of Adonis' where the 'perilous bough plucking' (*IP* 66) of Balder's 'thunder-besom' (*IP* 177) takes place.[10] These allusions supplement the suffering of the soldiers and lend an added disorder and conflict to their offensive.

At this point it may seem that the soldier's equation with pagan sacrificial ritual is ennobling or deifying, but in reality their sacrifice is a hollow one. This is evident when comparing the ritual destruction within Part 7 of *In Parenthesis* to 'The Hunt', another of Jones's fragments from *The Sleeping Lord*.

> stamen-twined and bruised pistilline
> steel-shorn of style and ovary
> leaf and blossoming
> with flora-spangled khaki pelvises
> (*IP* 170)

The above excerpt from *In Parenthesis* is matched by an extract taken from 'The Hunt'.

---

[10] Thomas Dilworth, *The Liturgical Parenthesis of David Jones* (Ipswich: Golgonooza, 1979), pp. 28-9.

for the thorns and flowers of the forest and the bright elm-
shoots and the twisted tanglewood of stamen and stem clung and
meshed him and starred him with variety
and the green tendrils gartered him and the briary-loops galloon
him with splinter-spike and broken blossom twining his royal
needlework
         and ruby petal-points counter
the countless points of his wounds

(SL 67)

'The Hunt' describes Arthur's ride against the Boar Trwyth in sacrificial terms that extend his suffering to epic proportion. The Boar Trwyth appears briefly within *In Parenthesis* when an artillery salvo is likened to the animal's progress that 'destroyed indifferently, men and animals, and the King's / son there' (*IP* 86). The Great Boar is a symbol of destruction in both 'The Hunt' and *In Parenthesis*, and requires a sacrificial ride to restore the devastated fertility, or in the words of 'The Hunt': 'for the healing of the woods' (*SL* 68). Through suffering with nature, and becoming that nature he suffers for, the destruction can be reversed. Arthur's 'palace wardrobe' (*SL* 67), like the 'flora-spangled khaki pelvises' of the British soldiers is 'gartered' and 'meshed' by 'twisted tanglewood' and 'stamen and stem'. In both poems abstracted grammar and enjambment merges cloth with 'bruised' (*In Parenthesis*) or 'broken' ('The Hunt') flora. This is then developed to encompass the body of the sacrificial man: the 'ruby-petal points' of Arthur's wounds and now the 'flora-spangled [...] pelvis' of the British soldier. Arthur is thus like the soldiers of *In Parenthesis*, not called 'Jack o' the Green' but 'the bleeding man in the green', a reference to the fertility rituals of *In Parenthesis* but also to *Sir Gawain and the Green Knight*. In this Middle English poem the Green knight allows Sir Gawain to behead him during a winter celebration that is ripe with seasonal imagery and pagan ritual practice, though ostensibly Christian in focus. In 'The Hunt' Arthur achieves a renewal of nature and the successful unification of all the splintered factions of the Island, but this sacrificial success is entirely missing from *In Parenthesis*. The alliteration and aural equivalence of '[b]rast, break, bough-break the backs of them, / every bone of the white wounded' (*IP* 178) conflates man and wood but does not bring renewal. The deaths of the soldiers do not carry revitalising balm, and their sacrifice does not bring healing to the forest; it simply accompanies the forest's destruction.

These sacrificial rites, both in 'The Hunt' and *In Parenthesis*, are paralleled by Christ's sacrifice. In 'The Hunt' Arthur's 'twisted diadem' (*SL*

67) connotes the crown of thorns, and his ride becomes 'the *Passion* of the Men of Britain' (my emphasis *SL* 69). The very last line, 'life for life' (*SL* 69), may be a reference to the myth of Odin strung upon a windy tree, a recurrent and powerful symbol to David Jones of Christ's crucifixion and its all-encompassing significance, both now and in the pagan past. 'The Fatigue' alludes to this myth when 'the Conqueror / . . . [hangs] himself to himself / on the Windy Tree' (*SL* 32); *The Anathemata* similarly makes mention of 'the windy tree' and 'Himself to Himself' (*Ana* 225); and then, with little variation, the lonely outlying trees of Beiz Copse in *In Parenthesis* suggest '[t]he hanged, the offerant: / himself to himself on the tree' (*IP* 67). The link between Odin and Christ is evident through reference to 'tree' or 'cross' as both the material and the generic shape suggest similarities.

The frontispiece exploits this visual equivalence by portraying a soldier awkwardly crafted into the cruciform with two trees in the near background mimicking the shape – perhaps the two thieves placed either side of Christ at Golgotha. Wood as crucifix is later suggested in an evocation of gallows construction when John Ball hears 'the noise of carpenters [...] which brought him disquiet more than the foreboding gun-fire' (*IP* 138-9). Indeed, the entirety of Mametz Wood becomes likened 'to the place of the skull' (*IP* 154). To a certain degree the soldiers even carry the sins and sufferings of others just as Christ did. When they begin the assault '[e]ach one [is] bearing in his body the whole apprehension of that innocent, on the day he saw his brother's votive smoke diffuse and hang to soot the fields of holocaust' (*IP* 162). These biblical and Christological references, similar to the pagan ritual allusions, elevate the soldiers' suffering to a mythical proportion.

Similar to the unfulfilled fertility rites however, the soldiers' Christ-like sacrifice is unsuccessful, or more specifically, perverted. The soldier's 'apprehension' of Abel's fear becomes bitter because they themselves enact the sin of Cain in taking up arms against their fellow man. Jones presents this fratricide in the form of Malory's 'Balin and Balan / embraced beneath their single monument' (*IP* 163) and in a later manifestation when 'Hansel with Gronwy share dog-violets for a palm, where they lie in serious embrace beneath the twisted tripod' (*IP* 185). The soldiers are not Christ even when they 'come in file, their lifted arms like Jansenist Redeemers, who would save, at least, themselves' (*IP* 169), for their outstretched arms are a perversion of Christ's universal forgiveness. Returning to the image of Cain and Abel, there appears the important symbol of a tree that also appears in the boast of Dai Greatcoat in Part 4. The 'green tree' (*IP* 79, 162), according to Paul Robichaud, is 'an allusion to Genesis mediated through Malory' in which a branch from the Tree of Knowledge is taken by Eve and planted outside the Garden of Eden.[11] It initially grew white until she had intercourse with Adam beneath it, at which it turned green, and the colour changed again when Abel was slain – this time to red in 'scarlet memorial' (*IP* 162). The 'green tree' is therefore burdened with its future discoloration, and with the sins of every soldier.

The 'green tree' appears one last time in a vision of tranquillity: a hospital with convalescing patients. The lingering of the forest, however, disrupts the quiet of the scene, and as the 'men walk [...] under the cedars / and by every green tree' (*IP* 186) the sin of Cain and the Passion of Christ is recalled. This moment of recollection finds parallel in the Prologue of *In Parenthesis*, a section of text taken from the *Mabinogion*.

> So he opened the door ... and when they
> had looked, they were conscious of all the
> evils they had ever sustained, and of all the
> friends and companions they had lost and of
> all the misery that had befallen them, as if
> all had happened in that very spot; ... and
> because of their perturbation they could not
> rest.
>
> (*IP* xix)

Derek Shiel writes movingly that 'Jones had experienced warfare as a soldier and relived it in the writing of *In Parenthesis*', just as the soldiers of the *Mabinogion* relived their sorrows by recounting them to others.[12] Jones's poem is therefore the anamnesis of his war experience. To Jones the word anamnesis is vital to understanding art but he found the dictionary definition of the word unequal to its religious significance. In *The Anathemata* he uses the following quotation to properly account for the word: 'in the scriptures of both the Old and New Testament *anamnesis* and the cognate verb have a sense of "recalling" or "re-presenting" before God an event in the past so that it becomes *here and now operative by its effects*'[13]. Though *In Parenthesis* is enclosed within the sleeves of its jacket, and though Jones asserts that 'the war itself was a parenthesis' or demarked

---

[11] Paul Robichaud, 'The Undoing of All Things: Malorian Language and Allusion in David Jones' *In Parenthesis*', *Renascence: Essays on Values in Literature* 53:2 (Winter 2001): 149-166. P. 159.

[12] Derek Shiel, 'David Jones: Making Space for the Warring Factions' in *David Jones Diversity in Unity*, ed. Belinda Humfrey and Anne Price-Owen (Cardiff: University of Wales Press, 2000), pp. 107-15, p. 111.

[13] Grigory Dix, *The Shape of the Liturgy* in David Jones, *Ana*, p. 205n.

space, there remains the ever occurring memory of the suffering, bringing David Jones to conclude in his Preface with an uneasy phrase: 'how glad we thought we were to step outside its brackets at the end of '18' (*IP* xv). 'Thought' is no release but a blurred boundary where the pain and suffering of the Great War seeps into the present. This failed closure is evident in the reappearance of the forest in Jones's other poems, and how that forest is symbolic of suffering.

Some peace and consolation does appear to derive from these trees however, or more specifically, *the* Tree. 'Mother of Christ under the tree / reduce our dimensional vulnerability' (*IP* 177) the cry comes. Mary under her tree – or cross – matches the trees of Mametz Wood where 'under each a man [is] sitting' (*IP* 184). The cry for protection turns each tree into a crucifix, and every soldier, like Mary, into a witness of the sacrifice of Christ. In a letter to René Hague Jones writes that 'all our miseries and sufferings can be seen as in some way part of the whole anabasis and passion' of Christ.[14] The trees under which the soldiers rest then, as well as signifying the turmoil of Cain and Abel, and the warring spirits of the wood, also signify the cross, but it is not to deify the soldiers, for they are inconsistent Christ figures just like the Jansenist Redeemers with their restricted forgiveness. Instead the soldiers contribute to the sins Christ bore, not giving redemption but receiving it. In discussing *The Anathemata* Jones wrote that 'I had occasion to consider the Tree of the Cross as the axial beam round which all things move.'[15]

The importance of the Cross takes dramatic form in *The Anathemata* when the poem's trajectory is surrounded by the offering of the mass, from the lifting of the 'efficacious sign' (*Ana* 49) to 'the Axile Tree' (*Ana* 243) of the last line. The Tree or 'dreaming *arbor*' (*Ana* 240) is not only the Cross but a reference to the Cross mediated through two poems: *The Dream of the Rood* (an Anglo-Saxon poem) and the *Vexilla Regis* (an early Latin hymn).[16]

---

[14] Quoted by René Hague, 'Myth and Mystery in the Poetry of David Jones', *Agenda* 15.2-3 (1977), p. 64.

[15] David Jones, *Epoch and Artist, Selected Writings by David Jones*, ed. Harman Grisewood (London: Faber and Faber, 1959), 39.

[16] *In Parenthesis* is striking in the absence of these two literary works (*The Dream of the Rood* and the *Vexilla Regis*) from its literary heritage, especially when it appears that the Anglo-Saxon poem was read to David Jones 'in the 1930s' by a cousin of his, and how he spoke of its 'marvellous' sound: David Jones, *Letters to William Hayward*, ed. Colin Wilcockson (London: Agenda, 1979), p. 71. Though David Jones heard it in the 1930s I am assuming that the exact date did not coincide with the writing of *In Parenthesis* for such a key influence to Jones's theory of the Cross's centrality would surely not have been omitted. Also see *Ana* 240n: 'Cf. the Good Friday Liturgy, the hymn *Vexilla Regis*, '*Arbor decora et filgida Ornata regis purpura.*' Tree beautiful and shining, made ornate with royal purple.'

Together the poems act as a mutually supportive palimpsest where Celtic and Latin traditions of Christianity are syncretised, symbolic of the unifying results of the Cross. Unlike the warring branches of 'numina' these different cultural responses to the Cross are harmonious and mutually edifying. Here alone can peace and comfort be found.

The recurring image of the forest and the suffering that takes place there intimates lingering trauma. This cannot be definitively claimed, but nonetheless suffering is inherent within these images from the sacrificial ride of Arthur in 'The Hunt', to Clitus's dream prophesying his friend's death, and to the continual focus upon Christ's suffering on the cross. The forest and the allusions made about the forest do not, as Fussell writes, 'ennoble' the soldiers who fight in it, but it does give them a humanity through their suffering, made both painful and powerful by the allusions that accompany it.[17] The Cross alone, whether signified by a tree in the forest or through evocations of Christ's sacrifice, is the redemptive symbol of peace within Jones's work, not eradicating suffering, but giving hope.

---

[17] Fussell, *The Great War and Modern Memory*, p. 158.

Anne Price-Owen

'Cook's Battlefield Experience Tours'

Mametz: a site-specific performance, by **Owen Sheers**, directed by Matthew Dunster, designed by Jon Bausor, with advice from Colin Hughes, Great Llancayo Upper Wood, Usk, performed by National Theatre Wales, 24 June – 5 July 2014

Most impressive in this evocative, innovative drama are the splendidly choreographed performances and the clever staging which creates close audience involvement, even a certain voyeurism as the audience listen in to private conversations and snippets. Cleverly conceived by poet Owen Sheers, who appropriates David Jones's *In Parenthesis*(1937), together with Llewleyn Wyn Griffith's *Up to Mametz – and Beyond* (2010). It is an intriguing mix of soldiers' movements and dialogues that match and meld with those of family members at home, as well as BBC reporters, typists in Whitehall keeping records and statistics, and other events which occur at the same weft and confused mayhem of time.

The support trench, constructed from materials and equipment found on the farm site, is not dissimilar to the trenches on the 1916 Front line. But that anticipated reality of the past surrenders to another present and we are thwarted! WWI soldiers writing letters home, attending to rifles, or making tea, unexpectedly morph into those who are clad in contemporary British Army uniforms: one listens to hip-hop music from a speaker attached to an iPhone, while another skypes with his girlfriend on an iPad. An army padre talks to himself in Welsh, and then, above the trench is a bespectacled man in an old fashioned suit and bow-tie who turns out to be the Dutchman Willem De Sitter. He clutches a pocket watch and, standing at a telescope on a tripod, cries, 'No hurry. Plenty of time. Plenty of time.' The significance of this is that the play is conceived as a diachronic structure, not one that operates synchronically.

Naturally bewildered, as were the troops in 1916, we are ushered into a milking barn, adapted to resemble an estaminet, a makeshift French café, where soldiers relax. Some dance with the local girls, some write letters or jape and argue among themselves. Our tour guide, 'Prof Phillips', hoisting his rolled umbrella high, welcomes us to Picardy, 1916, 'an area where the fields are already nourished by the blood of Welsh soldiers at the respective battles of Agincourt and Crecy.' And we reflect on the repetition of history.

The Prof ominously informs us that this is where another bloody battle will devastate this land, and by soldiers who had never even engaged in a large-scale attack prior to the forthcoming battle.

Phillips also reminds us that this 'will be a uniquely literary battle', because Officers Siegfried Sassoon fought in the front line prior to the onslaught, and Robert Graves was there in its aftermath. Two warriors of the 15th Royal Welsh Fusiliers, Private David Jones and also Llewelyn Wyn Griffith were some of the first participating at the outset of the carnage, the two authors who were the inspiration for promulgating this drama.

This play is as complex as its intricacies, together with the connotations, allusions and parallels that Jones applies to *In Parenthesis*. In placing WWI soldiers in close proximity to those of the 21st century, Sheers infers that there is little distinction between them. By introducing De Sitter, who was extremely excited by the publication of Einstein's Theory of Relativity in 1915, where space and time are inextricably interwoven and interdependent, Sheers operates a similar space-time continuum, or rather ruptured, fragmented time-shifts in his script. The memories of both David Jones and Wyn Griffith intermingle, interrupt, coincide and dramatically interplay with the play's own dialogue. At times we recognize the narratives, if I may call them that, for these too are interrupted, intermittent and coil throughout the dialogues with Sheers's own sub-plots playing out what appear to be particular, often domestic, stories that pertain to individuals. However, keeping in mind the relativity of the space-time undercurrent, these domestic incidents, which are never trivial, are universalized. Like Jones, the universal shines out from the particular in Sheers's writing.

In the barn that is the mainstay of the drama, we cannot make sense of what is going on – with the provocative oscillation between the popping up of different characters appearing on stage, a trench, or within windows of the house at right angles to the trench, facing the audience, and the mutant time/times factor. Like Jones and Griffith, it's on reflection that the whole story is constructed, deconstructed and reconstructed, albeit sporadically. In this sense, the play functions like a movie where flashbacks, or alternatively, future images may fuse in one continuous sequence.

This photographic theme is threaded throughout the action, perhaps a comment on the negative being transformed to a positive. A hinged opening at the back of the trench is called an aperture, whereby we get glimpses of the wood in the distance, and which accommodates the ear-splitting crescendo of shells, which are more muffled when the aperture is closed. Moreover, the camera has the subject covered in its lens, yet the subject is exposed by the resultant image. Covered/exposed is a further sub-theme in Sheers's play on words and actions. In photographic research, the veracity of the photographic image is challenged, because the print can be cropped, altering and skewing its context. Today, manipulation and mutilation are easily disguised by engaging with digital techniques to distort and transform the picture. Finally, the image assumes a moment frozen in time, but as we now know, time is a figment, a mirage, so it cannot stand still.

At one point, the private soldier David Jones appears firstly with a group of soldiers, before identifying himself, with his three comrades, as those with pathetically short pasts, who typify the common soldier. Together the four comrades are the composite of Jones's eternal Everyman, and universal soldier,[1] comprising Dai, who joined up to escape the dangers of the coalpits, Ellis, the Cardy milkman in London who found a white feather in a returned empty milk-bottle, and Aneurin who enlisted before he met his sweetheart from Llandudno, and then regretted his decision. Jones's fellow poet and friend, Saunders Lewis, who had fought in the Great War as an officer, suspected that:

'... Jones would admit to two impressions that grew into part of his make-up. First that the soldier is the normal Western layman, the chap who has always been there when the Graeco-Latin civilization of the West has had its quarrels or has had to be defended. Anonymous, unknown, peasant or small town labourer, he sailed with Odysseus, he fought at Phillippi, he was at the Milvian bridge, he was at Agincourt, he was a Desert Rat. He carries the traditions of three thousand years. He is timeless, old soldiers never die ... secondly, private soldier and Mother earth belong to each other with an intimacy that not even the shepherd can know. He befouls her, he digs her, he sleeps on her, he lies on her in action and inaction, wounded and unwounded, alive, dying or dead. She is ... the Mother, and there's an invocation to her in ... *In Parenthesis* where the battalion goes over the top[2]:

> ... mother earth
> she's kind:
> Pray her hide you in her deeps
> she's only refuge against
> this ferocious pursuer
> terribly questing.
> Maiden of the digged places
>   let our cry come unto thee.
> *Mam*, moder, mother of me
> Mother of Christ under the tree ... '   (*IP*, 176-7)

From 7 July, 1916, which is characterized by a steady rumble of artillery, the war takes on a menacing sensation that we associate with the arrival of machine-guns, gas and tanks. From here, the scenes tend to morph into one another, and the tension increases as the noise of grenades and bombs, if not constant, is anticipated. All the fevered attacks on Mametz wood arrive with a rhythmical regularity, and our affection and fears for the characters are as intense as they are visceral.

A further attack is duly set for the 10th July at 4.10am, and David Jones effectively pitches his voice level above the relentless noise of war, quoting directly from *In Parenthesis*. There are other instances of David Jones's voiceover with direct short quotes, some from *In Parenthesis*, some from Sheers, whose poetic elegance is poignant. Were it not for their subject matter, these musings might seem excessive at times in their lyrical poeticism.

As the barrage and shells cease, the faint sound of Welsh voices singing 'Lover of my Soul' to the tune of Aberystwyth grows to a crescendo, and then, silence. A section of the trench wall is removed, and the RWF go over the top, to take 'the dark wood'. We, the audience, in the thick of it all, don't know what to expect either, as we also are marshalled over the top, and down the chalk cliff to the field between us and the wood. That field is now a radio field of neon red telephone wires suspended in a grid of wooden posts, that narrows as we approach the wood. The noise from shielded speakers from the sidelines, is almost unbearable.

As we follow the regiment across No-man's-Land (in the darkening twilight), a group of women emerge from the wood bearing placards, and walk towards us and, mingling with us but going in the opposite direction to the wood, protest against the war, pleading for the lives of their sons, just as, in 2002, millions of us demonstrated our feelings concerning the proposed military campaign against Iraq. The machine-gun fire all but extinguishes the women's voices.

As we stumble and pick our way to the wood, we note vignettes of selected acts which the earlier sections of the play anticipated, perhaps parallel is more accurate: two rugby players running and falling, a mother washing her dead son, a couple making love for the first time, a Welsh and German soldier bayoneting each other, a dead German soldier reciting Graves's 'The Dead Bosche', and the messenger, Pte. Watcyn, running round in circles.

And all around us the broken and ineffective neon telephone wires are out of kilter. They dangle and lurk unsteadily in a rough circle that demarcates the action and inaction in this threatening space where the trees are festooned with vestiges of the conflict that the survivors, the dead and dying endured. Large photographs of the slain Welshmen are scattered throughout the wood, and the sizes of these images alludes to their heroic scale, a status the soldier earned among the trees.

Wyn Griffith gives his contradictory account of the carnage in the wood where 'there were worse sights than corpses. Limbs. Mutilated torsos ... a detached head ... So much red against the green. One tree ... held a severed leg its torn flesh hanging over a spray of leaf ... Past and future were equidistant and unattainable.'

As if to mimic Griffith's observations on past and future, and in the disarray, distortion, deviation and disorder, they find themselves attacked by their own artillery in the battle's blinding muddle and inefficiency of this war. De Sitter analyses the action: 'forward *and* backwards ... After all, they are not safely buried in the past as we might think them to be. They live with us. So we must act in such a way as to make them right.' Which we have not done, as the perpetuation of skirmishes, conflicts and wars since the 'war to end all wars' at the outset of the 20th century, continue into the present and beyond.

After David Jones has been shot in the leg, an older David Jones's voiceover considers abandoning his heavy rifle, as the drama is completed: 'Let it lie for the dews to rust it. Or ought you to decently cover the working parts. Its dark barrel, where you leave it under the oak, reflects the solemn star that rises ... from Cliff Trench. It's a beautiful doll for us, it's the Last reputable Arm. But leave it – under the oak. Leave it for a Cook's tourist to the Devastated Areas, and crawl as far as you can, and wait for the bearers.'

In this much fought-over wood, the prone bodies slowly get to their feet. They face the audience. The flash of a camera, the sound of an explosion, rings throughout Mametz Wood, and beyond.[3]

Notes

[1] David Jones's poem is shot through with liturgical, biblical and literary allusions that complement his text. By omitting these, Sheers eschews giving the soldiers a religious dimension and creed, thus ensuring the universal nature of the unknown, common soldier.

[2] Aneiran Talfan Davies, *David Jones: Letters to a Friend* (Swansea: Triskele, 1980), pp.115-6.

[3] All other quotations in the text are as they are written in the performance script. They do not follow the layout of David Jones's epic poem as in the Faber publication.

Martin Caseley

'The Unfathomable Deep': Negative Epiphanies and Loneliness in Edward Thomas' Poetry

i

Edward Thomas walks, once again, all around us: 'Adlestrop' is discussed in the quality newspapers, the war poems[1] are quoted regularly, the walks and cycle rides Thomas undertook are recreated on the radio and in print. Omniverous journalism, having explored all the well-worn tracks of the lives of Owen and Sassoon, increasingly turns its gaze to names like Thomas and Ivor Gurney. In addition to his poems, narratives of Thomas' life are inscribed within these discussions: the conflicted older man who enlists, the soldier who finds himself as a poet, the poet running from domesticity into the beckoning undergrowth of his death-wish. The centenary of 1914, the national discussion of just how this date is to be marked, together with widespread ambivalence about current conflicts, has all conspired to make the war poets our contemporaries once again. Revealing as much of this is, there is a surprising paucity of sustained recent critical comment on Thomas' poems and what they seem to be saying.[2]

The Ted Hughes quotation one keeps tripping over when thinking about Thomas is that he is 'the father of us all'[3]. A generous tribute, this perhaps needs careful evaluation. Thomas is not a mythographer, as Hughes can be, nor does he often exhibit the historical sweep of a Geoffrey Hill. He is divided from the natural order often enough, but not to the extent of a Larkin or a Duffy, or the panoramic vistas of Auden's gliding airmen. His world resembles the casual natural history essays of the Georgians often enough, but it is more charged and troubling, as I hope to show. Perhaps Hughes means in terms of Thomas' microscopic observation and recall of the natural world? On the other hand, the comment could be an anxious

---

[1] 'War poems' is problematic – relatively few Thomas poems *openly* reference the war, but it is everywhere implicit. 'In Memoriam', written in Easter 1915, marks the beginning of Thomas' explicit writing on this theme, though there are hidden currents also in 'Tears', dating from January 1915. All Thomas poems quoted can be found in Edward Thomas, *The Annotated Collected Poems*, edited by Edna Longley (Bloodaxe, Northumberland, 2008).

[2] There are exceptions to this generalisation: notably Glyn Maxwell's admirable *On Poetry* (Oberon Books, London, 2012) and some of Andrew Motion's writings on Thomas, in particular.

[3] Quoted in Maxwell, op. cit., p. 107.

realisation that Thomas' poetry casts a long shadow, discernible even against all the lengthening shades of war.

ii

Like many other facets of Edward Thomas, his patriotism is not easy to summarise, identify or, at times, empathise with, however much one may admire his poetry. As a journeyman hack, churning out prose books in the period 1906-1914, Thomas had plenty of time to hone his skill as a paid journalist. Under the influence of Richard Jefferies, the 19th century essayist, Thomas celebrated the pastoral charms of the Downs and Wiltshire. The titles of books such as *The Heart of England* (1906) and *The South Country* (1909) betray their contents: these are pages full of lists and lanes, woods, tracks and oast-houses. In the well-polished literary prose of his travels, there are many pictures of pre-war England, landscapes within which the figure of the poet can sometimes be discerned.

The essay 'This England', is typical of these. A description of walks taken with Robert Frost, it paints a suitably stirring, patriotic case for the Herefordshire landscape as a kind of kernel of everything he was to value and fight for. When printed in the November 1914 issue of *The Nation*, it probably found a sympathetic readership, and Thomas was later to quarry the poem 'The Sun Used to Shine' from it, recalling his walks from the vantage point of May 1916. History, names, the footpaths – the essay is quintessential Thomas, written before the poems started flowing from him. It is beautiful, lapidary – but strangely unnerving, too. The sun shines but there are 'dull sulphurous threats' from storm-clouds; there are 'black stooks' of beans, raucous rooks calling; the trees awaken thoughts of 'austere inhuman solitude'; there are 'wildly dark clouds' and 'shadowy elms'. Donald Davie saw this as a sense of 'loneliness' and described it as 'a psychological state which cannot find expression in any other way...both Thomas and Jefferies see something deadly in the non-human Nature that they celebrate'.[4] As one reads on, the atmosphere darkens and then comes Thomas' famous final paragraph: 'something, I felt had to be done', he states, feeling alienated and exiled from this paradise until he has fought for it. He admits to feeling overcome by thought, or 'something that overpowered thought', realising that his love was only aesthetic and, therefore, somehow unreal.

Crucially, after his encounters with Frost, Thomas finds another way to express the psychological pressures: in poetry. Frost maintained that this was really what Thomas was writing in some of his essays, and in this

---

[4] Donald Davie, p. 249, *With the Grain* (Carcanet, Manchester, 1998.)

particular case, the rhetorical raw material was already there in the essay. The images used in the poem – the purple-headed betony, the decaying apples – are present in the prose, but what the landscape stands for, as well as Thomas' response, is unknown, or Thomas is not yet willing to set it down. There is an awakening here, but it is paradoxical – the picture is composed, but Thomas is not. The long-sought answer can be tracked through the poems chronologically, arriving eventually at the explicit, unadorned 'Lights Out', but even before this, the epiphanies provided are often disturbingly negative.

iii

The early poem 'Old Man' sees Thomas beginning to explore these: ostensibly about memory, it moves from a family anecdote to the sudden depths of feeling revealed by Thomas' realisation that he has 'mislaid the key' and cannot unlock such memories in himself. A nihilistic fusillade follows, cancelling out garden, child, family until 'only an avenue, dark, nameless, without end' closes the poem as it narrows down Thomas' choices.[5]

Memory is also the key to 'Adlestrop', which has attained the puzzling status of the well-worn anthology poem, although to view it as just a nostalgic sketch of pre-war England is to undervalue the delicate way Thomas frames his pictures. There is an insistent emphasis in the first two stanzas of this brief poem, that it is 'the name' he recalls.[6] This is almost incantatory, eventually summoning up the long, tumbling list billowing out from the bare platform and taking up all of the final two stanzas. Synecdochically, this is a kind of reversal of the process described above in relation to 'Old Man': the doors eventually open and the moment is captured. Interestingly, however, Thomas' journal entry picks out the 'extraordinary silence' and the 'greater rustic silence' pooling out while the steam train stops.[7]

Rather than silence, however, the poem itself eventually dissipates in the misty sentiment of birdsong, with Thomas again engaged in naming places: 'Oxfordshire' and 'Gloucestershire'. The scene is set for an awakening of some sort, and Thomas searches the platforms and listens: his notes make it clear that he actually heard 'a chain of blackbirds songs'[8], but in the poem

---

[5] This is a first-person poem and the known biographical detail of the child and the door supports this.
[6] Thomas' mystical feelings about names can be seen elsewhere, notably in 'Words'.
[7] Given on p. 171 of Matthew Hollis' edition of the *Selected Poems* (Faber, 2011).
[8] Hollis, op. cit, p. 171.

this is pared down to a single blackbird, foregrounded nearby. For me, the immediacy of Thomas' scribbled notes disappears in some rather self-conscious effects: the adjective 'unwontedly' suggests something rare and unusual, yet the notes clarify that it is a perfectly routine stop while a signal changes[9]; similarly, the syntax in the third stanza becomes inverted and archaic ('no whit') in drawing a comparison between haycocks and clouds. Geoffrey Grigson, in a perceptive review of Thomas' prose, considers sentiment in 'Adlestrop' and notes that 'there isn't the clearest division between arousal of feeling and arousal of excessive feeling'[10]. These lapses into self-consciously 'poetic' devices gradually disappear in Thomas' later poems.

Compared to the carefully-selected landscape detail of 'The Sun Used to Shine' and the overwhelming rush of the nihilistic list which closes 'Old Man', however, the detail in 'Adlestrop' feels strangely incomplete – very similar to the raw material later 'worked up' by Thomas into books like *The South Country*. Popular and prized by anthologists as it is, it actually tells us very little: the power of the poem comes from the way it signals and taps into a deep mythical vein of 'Englishness', but one which Thomas barely gestures towards.

In the later 'Haymaking', Thomas explicitly depicts similar territory. Written nearly a year after the 'Adlestrop' journey[11], but printed in the 'This England' anthology[12] which Thomas edited for the Oxford University press in October 1915, once again he locates a moment of languor in the heat of the day: the labourers are 'still' and 'all are silent'. This pause, however, allows Thomas to move in a different direction to that in 'Adlestrop': here, instead of his vision moving outward from the train platforms across the counties, Thomas extends the rhetorical scope of the poem backwards through time. It becomes a portrait of an age, reaching back beyond John Clare and William Cobbett and all the components of the scene, until even the 'implements' are 'out of the reach of change'. To attain the composition of this picture, however, Thomas has to sweep in cinematically – down the empty road, past the mill-water, the wheeling swift, to the far end of the field – until he finally alights on the fine-grained daguerreotype of the

---

[9] It may be significant that the manuscript of the poem exhibits Thomas' second and third thoughts about this word: 'unexpectedly' was his first choice. Matthew Hollis finds 'unwontedly' exactly the right word – see the *New Statesman* of 15 August 2011, p. 53.

[10] 'Edward Thomas Again', collected in *Blessings, Kicks and Curses*, Geoffrey Grigson (Allison & Busby, London, 1982).

[11] This took place in June 1914; the poem was written in January 1915.

[12] 'This England', not to be confused with the earlier Thomas essay, also included 'The Manor Farm', both poems by "Edward Eastaway".

final ten lines. The concluding line of the poem summarises all of this as 'immortal', an interesting contrast to the rural task of haymaking with all the heavily-freighted symbolism of seasonal change it contains. To ensure this, however, the status of a mythical composition is necessary and in other poems, such as 'This is No Petty Case of Right of Wrong' the question of a future England, rising Phoenix-like, remains more of a generalised rhetorical feature, again ballasted by archaicism, this time with the imagery of witches' cauldrons.

iv

Rural labour provides the locus for the crucial discussion in the centre of 'As the Team's Head-Brass', written in July 1916. Here the creation of the picture is more elaborate, involving the full-scale framing device of lovers disappearing into a wood and later reappearing, but this is a piece of diversion on Thomas' part – the central thrust of the poem is contained in the discussion between the poet and the ploughman. We find that the immortal rural labour is no longer evident: it has met a similarly unstoppable force in the demands of the war. 'If he had stayed here we should have moved the tree' sighs the disconsolate ploughman, revealing that his mate has died in France.

The poem is constructed like a series of Chinese boxes: the outer frame is the lovers (signifying lyrical, dateless, continuity), the inner frame is the narrowing down of the ploughing (rural labour, immortal), but then we reach the centre of the poem and the fallen elm the poet sits on, felled by the 'blizzard' just as rural labour has died in the trenches. Even here, however, there is a certain amount of skirting around the unsayable: the ploughman reveals many have 'gone' (joined up) and are 'lost' (dead). How many? A 'good few', and even at this point it is the lack of vision the ploughman specifies in his final words: 'if we could see all all might seem good.' This careful, tremulous qualification recalls the way Larkin uses similar rhetorical techniques as ambiguous conclusions. The final four lines, introduced by the simple 'then', are a long elegiac sigh with the succession of 'crumble' / 'topple' / 'stumbling'. Larkin's 'The Whitsun Weddings' concludes with a similar dying fall: the sequence of slowing / tightening / swelling leads to the famous concluding 'arrow-shower' as the train pulls into London, and the possibility of fertility 'somewhere'.[13] In Thomas' poem, once again it is a nihilistic epiphany of destruction that is hinted at: the world of the ploughman, gestured at only a few lines

---

[13] Philip Larkin *The Whitsun Weddings*, (Faber, London, 1964).

before and already marked by change and sacrifice, will fall apart. The lovers reappear, largely to reinforce the framing device, but Thomas is left passively watching: there is nothing he can do (even after enlisting nearly a year before in July 1915) to prevent such change. Thomas Hardy's 'In Time of 'The Breaking of Nations''', to which this poem is a response of sorts, uses a similar framing device, but validates the lovers over and above the inevitable, unavoidable histories of war; Thomas simply gives us the reappearance of the lovers as one part of the rural world starting up again, after the pause occasioned by the conversation.

All Thomas can do, in fact, is embrace change, which he does in his last poems, such as 'Gone, Gone Again' and 'Lights Out', but really the time for exploring such epiphanies was over. In the former, the symbol of the old house, while still 'dignified' is already 'outmoded', and in the latter, loss ends everything, even the self. Elsewhere in Thomas' poems and prose, old farmhouses usually act as symbols of stability, but here even the temporary tenants have gone. Metaphorically blinded (the windows are broken), vandalised, it is the final summation of all the farmhouses populating the essays of Jefferies and Thomas himself. By September 1916, when this poem was written, the stillness of 'Haymaking' has given way to dereliction and abandonment: the grass grows, but significantly it now encroaches on paths, the human footsteps having all vanished. In the argumentative 'This is No Case of Petty Right or Wrong' Thomas had struggled to define why he was fighting, but as for the what, all he could offer was 'an England beautiful' rising with the Phoenix out of the ashes, secure on the level of myth, but lacking the precision and specificity of his earlier nature poems. For more convincing proof, one must return to the earlier 'But these things also', which modestly offers a list, in a minor key, of what that England would have to contain: new grass, snail shells, bits of flint, flocks of starlings – all the specificity of the earlier nature essays.

Edmund Gray

Laurence Binyon: War Poet and Much More

They shall grow not old, as we that are left grow old:
Age shall not weary them, nor the years condemn
At the going down of the sun and in the morning
We will remember them.

These lines of stanza four of 'For the Fallen' are very widely familiar, but Laurence Binyon, who wrote them, remains substantially unknown.

Binyon wrote the poem only six weeks into the war, not at its end as many assume, though he presciently foreshadowed feelings at the end of the war. The poem expressed a deep patriotism, which was kindled by outrage at the German infringement of Belgian neutrality and consequent sense that Britain must stand by its treaty obligations to go to that country's aid. His outrage was deepened by his devotion to the towns and people of Belgium, displayed, for instance, in his *Western Flanders* (1899), a prose meditation accompanying his friend William Strang's etchings, and by his friendship with Olivier Destrée, the Belgian writer on art and Benedictine monk, who was reported as killed by the Germans (falsely as it turned out). He was doubtless also shocked by reports of German atrocities (later doubted as propaganda fabrications, but recently confirmed by historians). He wrote the poem sitting beside his wife 'on the low cliffs of Polzeath', on the north Cornish coast, where they were holidaying with their three children, as they did several times – and where, as his grandson and literary heir, I had the privilege of unveiling a plaque in 2003. (There is as yet no Blue Plaque on the Binyons' London home at 118 Belgrave Road, where they lived from 1911 to 1919.) Binyon sent the poem first to *The Morning Post*, which rejected it, and then to *The Times*, which published it on September 21.

The poem embodied the patriotic fervour which swept across British society. We now regard the Great War as inflicting massive slaughter to little purpose, but this was not foreseeable in 1914. The rush to enlist was without precedent in British history, and affected writers, artists and musicians along with everybody else. Even natural dissidents, like Wyndham Lewis, fresh from his Rebel Art Centre and anti-establishment *Blast,* nevertheless soon volunteered (incidentally, with his commission papers signed by Binyon); and such very unmartial characters as Ford Madox Ford did so too. The high patriotic fervour which had already characterised Binyon's 'Fourth of

August' (printed earlier in *The Times*), also colours the third stanza of 'For the Fallen':'They went with songs to the battle... straight of limb, true of eye, steady and aglow,/ they were staunch to the ends against odds uncounted,/ they fell with their faces to the foe'. This has been criticised as remote from the reality of the war, but I think was not inapt to those who had set off at the outset of the war to fight courageously in the mobile withdrawals in the face of a far more numerous enemy at Mons and the first battle of the Marne.

The patriotic fervour was particularly striking in Binyon's case, because he was a man of pacific temperament and strongly anti-nationalistic. As a student, for instance, he had supported the motion that 'the principle of nationality is pernicious'; and much of his life's work was devoted to promoting understanding of other cultures. He would have liked to have enlisted himself, as he said in letters to more than one friend, but at forty-five he was too old. However, he devoted his summer holidays to service as an orderly in the Château d'Arc, in Haute Marne, a Red Cross hospital for French soldiers. Here he endured hard conditions and came close to the horrors of the war. His poem 'Fetching the Wounded' records one task; he assisted at operations, including 'dreadful' amputations; he also performed the humble tasks of housework and learnt how to construct bedside tables for patients. But his sense of humour did not desert him. One of his stories, handed down the family, concerned the ward sister who condemned the bed-making of a fellow volunteer in the tones of a Lady Bracknell: '*Disgusting*, Mr Fisher*'. He was deeply impressed with the fortitude of his patients. In 1916 he volunteered again, this time having to help cope with the torrent of wounded from the battle of Verdun. In 1917, however, the Red Cross assigned him to report on the work of British volunteers to all types of war victims in France. This resulted in a book, *For Dauntless France,* published in 1918, and praised by John Hatcher, the author of the excellent biography of Binyon, as ranking with 'For the Fallen' and 'Fetching the Wounded' as a 'major contribution to the non-combatant literature of the Great War'.

Back in London, Binyon served in the equivalent of Home Guard detachments – at different times on the top of the arch at Hyde Park Corner, in Holland Park and adjacent to the munitions factory in Woolwich, where his wife did night-shifts in the canteen. By the end of the war he had risen to the exalted rank of Lewis Gun Corporal.

The solemn, almost liturgical phrasing of the poem has suited quotation from it at memorial services and on countless war memorials, which have made the poem, though not its author, so widely known all over Britain, and also around the Commonwealth, a notable example being the New Zealand National Monument, where the words are inscribed on a massive flat disc with water flowing over it. Typically, it was intoned this year at the international commemoration of D Day held on the coast of Normandy. Testimony to its wider reach was its recitation by Mayor Giuliani of New York, at the 2008 commemoration of the victims of 9/11.

The much-quoted fourth stanza is undoubtedly the best part of the poem, with its echoes of Shakespeare and the King James Bible, and the contrasting brevity and simplicity of the last line which gives it such strength. The poem as a whole has been criticised for a tone of classical stoicism which offers little consolation to the bereaved, but there is ample testimony to the contrary. For instance, Kipling, who bitterly mourned the death of his son, was recorded as thinking it 'the most beautiful expression of sorrow in the English language'. It also says much that the British Legion quickly gave the poem a central place in their annual remembrance ceremony.

Elgar empathised with Binyon's war poems and set three out of the large number to form *The Spirit of England*, now recognised, after a period of neglect, as a considerable work in his oeuvre. When two of its sections were performed in 1916, a wounded officer, while attacking 'all the people writing about war & soldiers when they haven't a notion of either', considered Elgar and Binyon 'to express the feelings of non-combatants in the most touching & poignant way imaginable'. Binyon was indeed very aware of 'the horrible cost in pain, desolation, and waste' of the war, but retained his idealistic patriotism to the end.

It must be stressed that Binyon was much more than the author of the one poem. By 1914 he had already published eighteen books of verse. As a scholar at Trinity College Oxford, after St Paul's School, he had won the Newdigate Prize and was one of the four authors of *Primavera*, published by Blackwells in 1890. He was much influenced by Arnold and by Bridges, whose metrical skills he emulated. While still an undergraduate he became immersed in the group of nineties London poets and artists such as Lionel Johnson, Walter Crane, Frank Brangwyn and Arnold Dolmetsch, who were centred on the Fitzroy Street premises of the *Hobby Horse* journal, edited by Mackmurdo and Horne, which included a poem of his in its first number. At the gatherings there, he could observe Wilde 'talking brilliantly' and Yeats 'dreamy but fascinating'.

His *London Visions* of 1896 established his reputation. It was imbued with a strong sense of social concern, inherited from his father, an Anglican clergyman, and from his Quaker ancestry. 'The little dancers', describing slum children, has often been anthologised.

From 1895 he worked in the Prints and Drawings Department of the British Museum, where he launched his long series of art books with a catalogue of English Watercolours in 1895-1907, which is still a basic tool. The Print Room was something of a literary as well as artistic oasis under

Sydney Colvin, the friend of R.L. Stevenson. Many of the same people also gathered for lunch at the nearby Vienna Cafe where Binyon was at the centre of a grouping which included some denizens of Fitzroy, but also younger people such as Newbolt and Masefield. There he made the fruitful introduction of Ezra Pound to Wyndham Lewis, both men being amongst many he encouraged at the outset of their careers. Others were Arthur Ransome, William Roberts and Isaac Rosenberg (who later wrote a remarkable letter to him from the trenches). Charles Holmes recorded that Binyon had 'a wonderful eye for the needs of a friend' putting them in the way of 'any little job that might be vacant, or be invented' by him. In this role he edited or instigated several series: the Shilling Garland (nine poets at an innovatory shilling apiece), the Little Engravers and the Artists Library (commissioning Roger Fry's first book).

Bridges observed that 'the thing about Binyon is his beautiful mind', while William Rothenstein noted that 'behind a shy and diffident manner was a rich, humorous and most human nature... quick to discern and to welcome unusual talent in others, who rejoiced in what was new and vital in literature and painting'. Pound reported that 'he seems to be one of the best loved men in London'; later, Dorothy Shakespear (Pound's future wife) wrote to Ezra that he 'surpassed himself' in a witty speech of welcome to Max Beerbohm in 1913. He liked to make up improbable stories about his friends, and in a similar vein claimed that his lawyer billed him for 'being out when you called, five guineas'. He was good with children, never talking down to them. An unaggressive person, it was known that if he took an adverse view, 'Mr Binyon reserved his opinion'.

The contrast with members of the Bloomsbury Group was pointed up years later by an encounter of my own. Leonard Woolf, on being told that what I particularly remembered of my grandfather was 'sitting on his soft knee', remarked: 'Soft brain too'. Far from soft-brained, in his books on art Binyon effectively extended public appreciation. From 1897 he wrote pioneering books on Cotman, Crome and Girtin, and important works on Blake and his followers such as Palmer and Calvert. He was also an influential art critic for the *Saturday Review* (1906-11) and *New Statesman* (1917-19). In 1908 his *Painting in the Far East* was the first book on the subject as a whole in a European language, followed by the popular book *The Flight of the Dragon* (in 1911, last reprinted in 1972). He believed that 'the unifying principle of all the arts is what we call rhythm'; that art should be such that 'each individual, however humble, feels that he has a share', and that only by aiming 'to create beauty in our lives and surroundings' would society be redeemed from joylessness and apathy.

Alongside a continuous stream of poetry, Binyon wrote several verse dramas, including two staged with impressive sets and costumes by his friend Charles Ricketts (notable also for book design and illustration and much else): *Paris and Oenone,* in 1906, and *Attila*, with leading actors, in 1909. Though respectfully received, they failed to escape the incubus of Shakespeare, which defeated his aim of speaking 'to Everyman'.

In 1924 and 1928, came his most ambitious poems: *The Sirens,* which explores mankind's 'questing spirit' and *The Idols*, which deals with the obstacles to spiritual values. As long odes in traditional form and language, they have been bypassed by Modernism, though they dealt with such modern subject matter as the exploits of Mallory and Irvine – and at the time they were highly praised, and sold well. 'As great a poem as this century has produced' was a representative accolade for *The Sirens*, from Darrell Figgis in the *Sunday Times*. Binyon's *Collected Poems* of 1931 were the occasion of similar praise. Gordon Bottomley, for instance, declared that the book 'placed him among the major British poets for good'.

After retiring in 1933, Binyon's challenging project was a translation of Dante into English *terza rima*. This was highly esteemed by Ezra Pound, who regarded Binyon as having finally freed himself from 'the dogbiscuit of Milton's rhetoric'. It achieved its widest circulation in America, where it was available as a paperback. In Britain, however, it was only issued as three successive hardbacks, with the Italian on facing pages, and suffered competition from the more accessible Penguin Classics translation by Dorothy Sayers. This was slightly offset by a broadcast of the complete work in the great days of the Third Programme and more recently by import of the American edition, first by Chatto and then by Agenda Editions (in which it is still available). In the 1930s Binyon also helped organise verse-speaking festivals in Oxford, being a strong believer in poetry as a spoken art.

By 1939 Binyon's poetry had become 'simpler, less rhetorical and with a metrical fluidity which enacts rather than describes the subtle inflections of thought and language', as Hatcher puts it. Thus 'In Hospital', a poem in *The North Star* of 1941, could be praised as 'very fine indeed' by Spender, as a Modernist of the 1930s. The finest work of this late flowering was undoubtedly 'The Burning of the Leaves'. Musing over an autumn bonfire in the garden of his old Berkshire farmhouse in 1942, only months before his death, Binyon sounds an elegiac note of resignation, but also one of hope. The autumn bonfire is a metaphor for the relegation of vain things while the prospect of fresh resurgence concludes the poem – asserting that amidst the ruination of the war 'Nothing is certain, only the certain spring'.

Edmund Gray wishes to record his indebtedness to John Hatcher's *Laurence Binyon, Poet, Scholar of East and West* (Oxford, 1995).

N. S. Thompson

Anthologizing The Great War

According to the editors of a previous anthology of First World War poetry, over thirty British anthologies of war poetry were published between 1914 and 1918, the first within months of the outbreak of hostilities, when already the conflict was being called – almost prophetically – 'the Great War'. In *The Winter of the World: Poems of the First World War* (Constable, 2007), Dominic Hibberd and John Onions provide a good many similar statistics in their introduction and select over 120 poets out of the 2,225 British writers that Catherine Reilly listed in her *English Poetry of the First World War: A Bibliography* (1978). The poetry in the latter anthology is arranged year by year and is intended as a historical reflection of the range of verse published rather than a critical perspective that selects the best on the grounds of literary merit, as previous editors had done. They did this in order to debunk three myths: that war poetry was written only by soldier poets, that it was only on the front line that these poets began to lose the spirit of patriotic duty and rebel against the fighting and, lastly, as a reminder that it was poets other than the ones celebrated today who were in favour at the time. Thus in 1917, Captain P.H.B. Lyon can write with undiminished emotion in 'Comrades in Arms': 'Not ours the zeal that passes with the years/ The will too faint to battle with desire;/ In the dim twilight-time of doubts and fears/ Our lips were singing and our eyes afire'.

It is instructive to see the best of Great War poetry in the context of this kind of verse. And it is surely too easy to despise it, given the circumstances of its composition. Nevertheless, if we want to understand why great poetry is great poetry then it often does require a 'look at the worst'. In the same way, it is easier to understand why Shakespeare enjoys the reputation he does if you have read (or dipped into) *Gammer Gurton's Needle* or *The Shoemaker's Holiday*.

The Winter of the World, then, was an interesting historical exercise. Whether one would wish to have it on the bookshelf is another matter. To date, that place has been occupied by such popular anthologies as Brian Gardner's *Up the Line to Death* (1964), I.M. Parsons's *Men Who March Away* (1965) and Jon Silkin's *The Penguin Book of First World War Poetry* (1979, 1981). The first two of these reflected a renewed interest in the poetry stemming from the satirical musical *Oh! What a Lovely War* (1963; and later a film, 1969), which portrayed the powers behind the war in a cynical light, reflecting the general rebellion against authority of the 60s. Although

Jon Silkin's edition included no popular song, he brought together for the first time several international voices, including those of the opposing side (Georg Trakl, Ernst Stadler, August Stramm, among others) and voices from France (Apollinaire), Italy (Ungaretti), and Russia, including Anna Akhmatova and Marina Tsvetayeva, especially in the expanded second edition.

Much has happened since those years to expand our knowledge and correct errors of chronology. There has been an anthology of women's poetry, Catherine Reilly's *Scars Upon My Heart* (1981) as well as critical studies, and Vivien Noakes edited *Voices of Silence* (2006), a fascinating anthology of what might be called the many unpublished 'inglorious Miltons' who – despite the paradoxical title – were far from mute.

With so much information (and so many anthologies now published), what can an editor do today to make a viable contribution? For some years Tim Kendall has made war poetry his subject and, with Philip Lancaster, is at present editing *The Complete Literary Works of Ivor Gurney*. As a result, his *Poetry of the First World War: An Anthology* (Oxford University Press, 2013) is a quality production in terms of both format and content and manages to tread a careful line between inclusiveness in its range of voices and excellence in terms of the poetry. Obviously there will be few surprises, apart from several previously unpublished works by Gurney, but the whole is put together with an almost narrative force that makes it coherent and compelling. In all, the number of poets is a manageable twenty seven, plus a group of 'Music Hall and Trench Sons' to conclude. If we can rightly expect the usual suspects in Blunden, Graves, Owen, Rosenberg and Sassoon, it is refreshing to see non-combatants such a Wilfred Gibson given a generous inclusion. And whereas Jon Silkin saw fit to asterisk (almost with a literary health warning) the poems he felt obliged to include because they were 'loved' by many readers, Kendall has no such prejudices. He is happy to include Julian Grenfell's 'Into Battle', Charles Sorley's 'All the hills and vales along' and Owen's 'Anthem for Doomed Youth' without any quibbling. However, we do not find John McCrae's 'In Flanders Fields', nor Alan Seeger's 'Rendezvous'. There are generous selections from the women's camp in the familiar work of Mary Borden, May Wedderburn Cannan, Margaret Postgate Cole, Charlotte Mew and May Sinclair, but surprisingly no Vera Brittain. There are interesting short appearances from Laurence Binyon, Robert Service, T. P. Cameron Wilson, Patrick Shaw Stewart and Arthur Graeme West among the less well known, prefaced by the literary greats of the time whose selections introduce the volume: Hardy, Housman, Yeats and Kipling.

What makes this anthology invaluable is the attention to detail. Not only is there an acutely perceptive general introduction, but all the poets – including the often misunderstood Rupert Brooke – receive a sympathetic and well judged individual introduction, together with a wealth of biographical and bibliographical information. Although no particular audience is specified in the introduction, some of the explanatory notes do seem over scrupulous to an English reader, especially where English geography is concerned, but then the demands of an international readership may be the reason. Scholars and critics will be grateful for accurate dates and texts given as well as for the literary allusions and references.

In the introduction to his Penguin anthology, Jon Silkin was much concerned with how his selected poets were grouped together (indeed, later editors happily used thematic titles) and felt he had to justify one particular pairing:

> ...the grouping of Sassoon and Owen is meaningful. They share a vision of realism, a concreteness and specificity, in confronting the horror of trench combat...   (p.51, second edition)

I would say that the reason for our continued interest in the poetry of the Great War (to use its original name) is precisely because the poets (and prose writers, who were often one and the same) were able to write with such realism, concreteness and specificity in literary terms, over and above the horrors (and the pauses in horror) they witnessed and depicted. They provide a lesson in concision and lack of flummery and were able to use imagery in a deftly effective way that was no ornament but tellingly functional. Tim Kendall's anthology will provide the best critical introduction to their body of work as its authority and accuracy supplants previous anthologies.

Gill Learner

Aunt Emily wanted to be a Boy

Her brothers taught her to kick a ball and ride a bike,
to fall and climb back on. That August day when George
set sail in naval blue, Tom cursed his youth
but she enrolled. Once across she'd cut her hair,
steal khaki kit, slide into a line of marching men.

So she served her apprentice months in hospital –
scrubbed floors, held her breath for bedpans,
laundered bandages. Her feet felt bastinado'd, hands
lost their lily silk. She padded splints, coaxed soup
into helpless mouths, lit their cigarettes.

In France at last she wiped away blood and mud
to reveal the boy beneath, held shaking hands,
leaned on shoulders as rags of serge were peeled
from mangled limbs, bathed men too weak to wash,
tried not to look at defenceless genitals.

Bedpans didn't matter after rotted flesh. Lack
of sleep was nothing to the wildness in men's eyes.
Somewhere between home and the glint of metal
embedded in a chest, bravado turned to shame:
'Thank God,' she said, 'I never fired a gun'.

In Coventry, 1940-1962

It wasn't a reforming king, or time's unkindness, but
a night-raid by the Luftwaffe, and seven centuries
of prayer were blown to dust. Without bitterness
a vow to rebuild beside the broken stones rose
with the smoke. Sandstone was quarried, ferried,
layered into zigzag walls, glass screens were scratched
with saints and angels, windows reared up letting in sun
to colour-wash the marble floor, charred beams and
ancient nails became symbols of the faith.

A man who refused to kill was invited to write the score.
On a framework of the Requiem, he hung the verses
of a soldier from an earlier war. For the Latin he called on
men and women who'd seen their cities burn, boys
too young ever to have heard a bomb, and a soprano
whose Soviet countrymen had died in millions.
An English tenor and a German baritone sang Owen's rage
and grief in turn. Then at the last, against the consoling
orisons of choirs, they repeated the closing line in harmony:
Let us sleep now ...

Chris Hardy

No Boots in the Hall

After the cease-fire the widows and
the young and older unmarried women,
and the boys, the sons of the dead,
are left.
The boy children in the houses of women,
the villages of women,
the cities of women.
The boys, who will one day love
the widows' daughters,
do not know or care
what love is,
or that the doorways and the stairs,
the beds in their mothers' rooms,
are wider than they need to be.

Swiping each other with nettles,
sticks and rocks, and laughing,
falling into ditches
and leaping out, they run
through churchyards on their way
to school, where suddenly quiet
they stand in line.

The sons who will not defy their fathers
grow like saplings on a plain
newly stripped of forest.
Their mothers see the father
in the boy's face but
the man is dead
and the boy cannot replace him.

Donald Avery

Dormez-vous?

1915

In trench tonight
we dream we lie
where sheets are white
and pillows sweet
and blankets dry.
Will soon be light.
And time to eat –
and time to die.

God's help we need.
He does not seem
to hear nor heed –
His council keeps.
The while we dream
mayhap He sleeps.

Falling

Light as fall of
    aspen leaf,
light as footfall
    of a thief,
falls a memory
    on a grief.

Falls as blessing,
    falls as spell,
falls as wish in
    wishing-well;
falls as first in
    love we fell.

Angela Kirby

At The Imperial War Museum

(formerly Bedlam)

Mr. Softee has parked his van
in the shadow of the great gun
where the Bar-B-Q stall does a brisk trade
in charred meat.

One be-medalled veteran snaps
another who is standing to attention
between the twin barrels.

Inside, beneath the cupola, all is sepia, mud,
duckboards, gangrene and trench mouth,
a collage of faded photographs, diaries, letters.

Dear Madam,
I thought you would wish to know as how we found
the Brigadier's horse and are taking care of it ...
Gerry was still going for us so we had to leave
Lieutenant Blackshaw and twelve of the lads...

Dear Frank,
Just a note to tell you we went back again this year; not
many of us left now. I was standing next to the old General,
looking at the crosses, when he turns to me and you won't
believe this, Frank, 'What cunts we were, Sergeant,' he says,
nods, put on his hat and marches off. All the best, Harry.

Children charge headlong over flower-beds,
indifferent to the constant rat-a-tat of starlings
and sudden bursts of forsythia along the road as
they dodge the red bayonet spikes of cordylines.

On Anglesey

Certainly Rhosneigr, most probably August –
in my mother's hand, Picnic at the beach! 1928.
Ten years back from Gallipoli and the Somme,
six uncles lean against Lion Rock, captured
there by her Box Brownie, seemingly at ease, sun
warmed at the sea's edge, Gold Flakes in hand.

Look at them: their dapper white flannel trousers,
open-necked white shirts, blancoed tennis-shoes,
admire the neat moustaches. If you didn't
know better you might believe the smiles, forget
those shadows behind their eyes, the absence
of the youngest brother, that empty sleeve.

Mary Durkin

Glory Holes

This was not their war to tunnel to,
but quickly they came, from Durham, Lancashire,
from Kilkenny and Tyrone, from Welsh valleys,
the Ruhr valley and from Saarland
in the subterranean search for light,
for the sharp yellow glint of the canary.

The pitmen I knew were mild, even in drink,
loved dahlias, tended allotments, reared pigs.
By my grandfather's side, I was kept
from the other, roughened men tunnelling
through stone, sea, clay; caged, coughed up, soaked,
black, yet whistling still with the canary.

These men hewed hard, hoped hard,
bantam battalions waist-high in water, poison gas –
blasted, entombed. Those who escaped grey
in the clay and cold half-light, inched their way
home through noman's land; lost, listening
for the sweet, clarion call of the canary.

Michael Curtis

That's Me

on the right, waistcoat, watch chain, dicky bow,
jaunty grin under a cocked straw hat, shiny spats,
white suit, foot on a tree, out on a spree, that's me

with Alice at Blackpool, lounging in the window
behind her sisters, reading the card she sent me,
my lonely wife, when I was overseas, and that's

my uniform and stick, first time, spick and span,
keeping still for the photographer, and mother,
and there, in the middle, next to corporal, by our hut,

second bed on the left enjoying my Blighty
at the Wharncliffe, better than the ten day furlough
back in 1915, till it was time to go back again,

and that's me at the front of the Bible Class team,
with Desborough Town FC, white towel over my shoulder,
on the first row, 1949, for the United Counties Trophy,

there's Reggie Meen at the Old Temperance Hotel
when my own days in the hempen square were through,
me holding the ropes at the Tigers' ground in '31

in front of thirty-five thousand, when we took the title,
Empire Heavyweight, Larry Gains, Levene and me, that's
my boxing school, there's Ben Foord, another champion,

that's my shoe tree, unused leathers, gloves empty,
shrinking on a hook in the shed, there's my twenty-six years
at Crompton's, my fifty in the Boot and Shoe Union,

and there I am in the Garden, right by Alice, Section 9,
look closer, the roses are higher now, there, near the wall,
still fighting fit, tidy, well turned out. That's me.

Reuben

Many ways to leave this earth
big brother, tragic and absurd,
but this one stokes an anger
that keeps your death alive

as I scroll down the page
from census to headstone, read
Killed in Action in France, picture
you lost in a lethal attack –

Action? Helped a batman
unload the lieutenant's baggage
from the steam wagon, lugged down
the platform, dropped with relief

to explode you across October air
as the live fuses he'd packed
(thinking they had some worth)
performed their task, relieved

you of the bother of finding a berth
after Armistice a month later.

D.V. Cooke

In Memoriam – The Lost Country

(From a longer sequence published in its entirety in the online supplement)

On the Salient

Clapping you now the hands break bread,
Once steered the plough that cut the soil
That carved the land to harvest the dead.

These lands once were blood and earth that bore
And grew the wheaten field that nourished
The days and hands that went to war.

The war was trenches dug and attacked
At point of bayonet – and there
Like an angel lunged and fought and hacked,

And carved the war that made the lands
A barren waste. A blood-hewn contract
Has buried the day, yet once these hands

A rifle held and parried where men
Fired clip after clip into mounds
Of flesh till the breech grew hot and then.

The somnolent dead lay around.
Unbearable detonations – broken
Men in their own blood dying, drowned.

The soil remains – the soiled remains,
And over that torn yet fertile plain
The skull occasional the plough upturns.

In the Dugout

Duskily as if out of dream
The long line of trenchcoats come
Out of their lair and burrow, out of their
Mud-prolonged darkness; from earth
And death unbound. Yet summoned
From this rut and domain we squat
Or kneel in the saurian dark –
Mere ghosts of the men we were.

Or scuttle like insects though
Insects are colossal here – until we are
Denatured or resort to orisons. Gradually
The gun-demented roaring lessens or by
Degree increases. Who now remembers
Us – remember us as strained faces
That blossom amid darkness,
That tunnel these damp hollows.

Lullaby

Touched by the dawn's coruscating cry,
The ripening blossom trembled, fell,
And the guns, the wrangling guns they sigh
Over farm-house, orchard and dull canal.

Man here is but a turning weather-vane.
Yet who are these seen in silhouette –
These fading soldiery that trudge and sweat
Through vortices of an old campaign?

Under the flowering cherry – supine,
At ease they lie. Yet once inside a time
There we sang as light leapt to defend
And the guns gouged the honorific friend.

James Roberts

Woman at a Piano

The space is illuminated by fires stampeding soundlessly
    through buildings across the square. Shadows of
        stacked crates writhe.

The piano has been silent for years, wrapped in a hanging fog,
    the room filled floor to ceiling with dust.
        She touches the keys

lets her hands fall over an edge. The piano's fingers flex,
    the tendons obey and notes fan out
        like a bird set free

only to find itself in a bigger cage. She can hear feathers
    as it tries to escape through the walls to a red sky.
        The walls throw the notes

back weighed down with bricks, tinged with the colours
    of all that has penetrated their pores for centuries,
        the soft footsteps,

the dead languages. Outside bombs are falling silently through
    space. Buildings prepare to leap, burst, tear down.
        She hears it

the world breaking again, all voices failing to one scream,
    unfolding to be enveloped by this permeable stillness,
        to be shaped into a chord.

Stephen Claughton

A 2nd Lt, 20th Royal Fusiliers

By the time I knew him, he seemed impossibly old.
Tall and thin, always scrupulously correct,
he carried himself as if he were labelled 'fragile'.

His stiffness seemed inhibition as much as age,
the result, no doubt, of a strict, Victorian childhood,
always the stifling pressure to conform.

Music had been his rebellion: enrolment
in the Royal College, not varsity, then the living
he scraped as teacher and organist.

He played even in old age, practising each day
on the Bechstein upright he'd brought to live with us,
a black antique, complete with candle-holders.

The piano was old, but Grandfather was older:
already twenty-four when Victoria died,
he was almost too old to fight in the First World War,

but joined up anyway with the OTC, surviving two years
in the trenches, commanding a Lewis gun.
Promotion, he said, would have taken him 'over the top'.

When he married my grandmother, ten years younger,
she must have seen widowhood coming, regardless of war,
but the old man, a survivor, outlived her by twenty years.

She worried for both of them, my father said,
Grandfather carrying on insouciant as ever,
lack of ambition his best survival tactic.

I still have the postcards she sent him at the Front,
shadowy, monochrome views of the Yorkshire Dales,
which returned unscathed, when they invalided him home.

I wonder if, in his nineties, facing death again
– no armistice this time – he saw it as promotion
he couldn't decline, or at his age 'a Blighty one'?

What else would Elysium be but a version of God's own county:
limestone scarps, uplands grazed to a nap,
a curlew's bubbling cry – and somewhere a piano?

Edward Greenwood

August 1914 – In Memory of My Father

I often talked with you as you sat there
With the evening paper, as you always did,
And sometimes wished to speak of the campaign
In Flanders in that August. It was plain
To me that you, like many, might not care
To uncover things much better to keep hid.

Such questioning might make you once more lose
The peace that time had brought, to some dread sight
Of fear, of fatal wounds, of dying men.
You would not want such memories again
As calmly you took in a new war's news,
And folded up the paper, neat and tight.

To waken agitation time had stilled
Would only have been cruelty in me,
And I am glad now that I then took care
Not to recall the thoughts you'd rather spare
Of how men rose to kill or to be killed
And saw things no one should be forced to see.

S.K. Smith

Harry

Stark bloody-minded,
Dogmatic, moody,
Got through it somehow
He did.

Raw dragoon trooper,
Under-age farmboy,
Barrack-bred culture
Grew him.

Time-served, navvying
Shovelled off a lifetime,
Brute boots and Dubbin
Shod him.

Pensioned arthritis,
Claimed on the trenches,
Clasped up a hip joint,
Ditched him.

Slogged till it floored him,
Damned it and blasted,
Grudge-ridden lurcher,
Bore it.

Cheap parish digger's
Crude bit of spadework
Gritted his set teeth
For him.

Char March

Lest We Forget?

This quiet graveyard is now eulogised
as 'wildflower-friendly': Eggs-And-Bacon
thread through Ladies' Bedstraw and Self-Heal.

The Norman porch displays a list
of the ninety-two lichen taxa
Found by the enthusiastic British Lichen Society

including the rare Porpidia soredizoides.

We stroll through knee-high Yorkshire Fog
and Sweet Vernal Grass mouthing
the graves' names, their ages.

Turn a verdant corner and
come upon them: scoured,
buzz-cut, rawly new.

Do they want this regimented scrubbing?

This forever standing to attention:
All-ready-for-an-inspection-sir!
Why not let this 19 year old, this 22 year old,

this Private, this Lieutenant develop a skin
of lichen, a suit of moss, a softening
of bird-splatter?

Do they want their grasses and wildflowers
shaved to within a millimetre of their soil?
Does this six-monthly assault with electric sander

comfort them?

Or do they wish to rest, to lie
hammocked in the curve of the earth,
to become one with the bearded graves

that cluster round them, that lean in
like ears, like hands ready to soothe,
while the soldiers stand to attention

in uniforms stiff with bleach?

The Finding Of Parts

I believed my grandad
to be a sailor of The High Seas,
for, in my picture books,
only pirates had tattoos,

and scars. He played along
with my stories of the ink
blurs on his arms, *'Arr, Jim Lad.*
Doubloons and a purple parrot!'

Thirty years later, I found
the dusty box of tapes; got
the reel-to-reel machine
working again. Heard

my dead father's *'One-Two, One-Two'*.
Then granddad's gravel
spooling out: the quivering
candle in the dug-out;

the Quink Permanent in a tin mug;
the needle passed round;
the extra ration of rum;
the wincing of each lad.

All that week his platoon
had been on *Collecting Duty* out
in No-Man's – picking up
bits of their dead mates,

and failing to match them up.

So each unique design was scraped
into him by one of his KOYLI mates;
into each forearm, each bicep,
each calf, then torso, back, neck.

They'd each sat, bleeding, proud
they'd faced the pain; puffing
on Navy Cut. And then,
tongues pressed between teeth,

drew on the fly-leaf of their
1915 Soldier's Diary, each tat.
Here is the stick-figure he drew
– transfixed with arrows –

my grandad as St Sebastian.
At each arrow's flight-feathers
a cramped sketch that meant:
Private John Henry Taylor's

left forearm, right calf, ...

'It was summat we could do'
grandad crackles from the tape
sucking on his pipe, sucking again.
'So we could be...' A rattling cough.

'So all of us could be safely gathered in.'
And then there is his dry laugh,
and the tape – softly clattering
its red tail round, and round.

(KOYLI = King's Own Yorkshire Light Infantry)

Clare Best

Pahn Bari, 1919

All year she waits, all the monsoon weeks
when the piano drifts out of tune
and playing as she sings becomes an agony,
until she takes to the verandah
singing Schumann, unaccompanied, to the hills.
Once the men are gone to the tea garden
she sings, leaving the piano in its shaded room.

The day the tuner visits, late September,
thin mist on a grey lawn (Oh the relief
of cooler weather), she stands by a rose bush,
looks over her shoulder and seeing him
she thinks of another man she knew
across the ocean, long ago, who smiled,
unlacing his boots as he came in.

This man is beautiful. She admires
his lean hands around the glass of water
like a boy's. Hands to adjust hammers
and chamfer felts. Long fingers
for stroking keys. (Listen, the blush of silence
before skin touches ivory). She hears the hands
working, working on the strings.

Something about him makes the house shiver
into life – the coaxed piano tones,
and then his carefulness, the way he coughs,
inquiring *Has the instrument been shifted
in recent months?* His sips of water
between chords, right hand placing the glass
away from the keyboard, just in case.

While he tempers each interval
she teases notes from tangled notes.
In her dark head she knows them – and yes
she likes the discomforting closeness,
the way sounds overlap. Pure mathematics
in the fifths. Now and then, she thinks
she would like to work this miracle herself.

Clare Crossman

Back Fields

Not much, but it was where we crossed between
the houses. One gravel path over a scrubland
of grass, where most hurried to town
and no one minded about the dogs.

A small hill, we got to know it on tin trays.
Makeshift toboggans, flying down toward
the eel sheds and factories beside the sludge-filled
River Medway, with its iron bridge to Strood.

Face down we'd press our hands into the snow
until we saw the green. Hidden and wet,
like summer which seemed years away.
I fell and grazed my knees, stung clean with iodine.

We were shown how dandelions blow clocks
and daisies make a chain. I never learned to
sound a grass note from the single spike
threaded through my hands, but learned seasons,

the shape of ground under my feet; that
not everything is written by us. I could
not read the heavy memorial plaque riveted
to the entrance wall: Donated '1918

in memory of a fallen son.' Unbuilt on,
Backfields still hurtles children under the sky,
history held forever, in the grey stone walls,
that witness those who lived to walk the river.

A 1920s Childhood

(The Granby Hotel, Harrogate)

(For my father)

Outside the windows of the long hotel,
there are men and women queuing in the rain.
It does not seem like this when you run
along the corridor towards the kitchen
where the cook is making toast.
Your morning smells of breakfast.

From the back there's a view of allotments.
People dig all day and pick the sky-high beans
wrap them in newspaper, whistling.

You are told there has been a war.
Old men with broken faces covered
in tin masks are selling matches.
Your mother plays the piano everyday
because your father came home.

Luck has brought you here.
Your grandfather's ball-bearing eyes,
his aptitude for maths, his guesses
at the main chance.
You help fold the large white sheets.

The French governess, 'Madame'
comes every week. Her heels clack.
You must learn the language of travel,
French names for wine, the words the waiters speak.

You hang up damp overcoats
from the strangers who arrive in the rain,
are allowed to dress up as a chef
to serve stern men their dinners,
like in the silent films you go to with your brother.

You have a daily matinée,
are running down a modern tunnel
to where the European cities wait.
When you reach the light,
you will translate, another dark.

Christine McNeill

A day moving into night during World War I

He was alone in a crowd whose faces
were bright from warm sunshine.
In a flash, they fell.
And still that glazed ball of the sun;
none down in the mud, moved leg or hand.

He was one of them;
saw flies feasting on rotting flesh;
trees in vast forests felled;
head-scarfed women carrying firewood for heating.
Where the trees had stood for almost a century

grew lilies-of-the-valley – millions
with bowed heads;
lying on his belly in grass
he'd drawn a posy of them
on a field-card sent home.

Dear Love and *many kisses*.
Was it a dream from which he couldn't wake?
Rain pelted down, and a sunbeam from somewhere
he couldn't see lit his window –
the shadowed journey of raindrops across words.

He saw right through them to being
a boy in his mother's arms,
saw the image far off and as close as his hand –
a beginning, small and significant
as in all life stories.

David Cooke

The Grimsby Chums

They are swaggering down
Freeman Street, comrades-in-arms –
their steps buoyant with self-esteem
and a changed sense
of where they are from.

At their backs Icelandic bluster
has chivvied them along
from the dock end's rough banter
– its lacklustre backdrop
of estuarial grey –

toward Top Town's flags and brass.
Easy going veterans
of drink-fuelled brawl,
they'll sign up and knuckle down –
disciplined recruits.

And after endless nights
on far-flung fishing grounds
how hard can it be
to march in style
across some fields of beet

beneath vast sky
that seems familiar –
like the girls lining up
for any lad with a bob or two
and a lopsided grin?

David Mohan

Lusterware

Your dresser had polish –
the plates you kept
as lucent as ceramic moons.

They brought order
to your country cottage,
to the muddy back yard,

offering exemplums
in miniature scene –
Arcadia, Delft studies, Rome.

Beneath them you always
kept a clean cloth,
like a setting to places

farm life never touched.
Not when your daughter left –
the yard outside rutted

with wheel marks – your
husband scarred by accident,
you, losing breath, wired

to a machine, only too late
did your life match pictures,
the melt-steam of some kiln,

rising to cloud where you waited.
Colours ran, a blur, as though
some artisan shook his latest vignette,

seared by heat into the glaze of fact.

Geoffrey Heptonstall

Birds of Passage / Rites of Paradise

Cargoes on the waters rising
Where ships are sailing into mind
The ocean's gift of passage
Is surely instrumental
In the homeward unloading.
See the covey of masts.
On the horizon line.

Of paradise there are rumours
Floating feather-like in morning air.
Our waking eyes are brushed
By the wind that stirs the dust
As far as a mind can imagine.
All else is speculation
As distant as the night stars.

Now from eyes that can see
A summoning of elegant reflections
On certain doubts we may have.
Their words on waxen wings
Speak to heal the pain of things.

Harriet Torr

Remembrance Day

Remember the Xmas truce
how German lyrics floated
through the air
thick with gun smoke
which stuck to the skin
turned men blue,
but we laughed because
it was Christmas?

How fairy lights of shrapnel
lit up a tree's stump
as flesh tunnelled through
gangrene and pus
and hailstones pitter
against the shin
into the open mouths
of the dead?

How once the leadened sky
split open to reveal
the river's stones
sun shaped and simple
the broken body made whole.

Jennifer A. McGowan

Tyne Cot

Flint walls spark remembrance.
Portland stone foots a sea once more –
rank upon rank of immaculate tragedy.

Pilgrims are not what they once were:
no longer family, they take
a few rushed, desultory snaps, get their
high heels caught in the hex grid placed
to spare tourists the realism of mud.
Death is big business; cleanliness next to.

Mud was what they knew; still know.
More drowned in it than died of wounds.

If online diaries cannot give sufficient witness,
this wall, this here, this now, with its thousands of names –
the missing, the blown-to-bits –
curves into infinity. Rosebushes extend roots
into the heart. Lower your phone;
let this ocean wash over you.
Man was made from clay. Mud unto mud.

Juliet Aykroyd

Mabel Verdun Jones

No two days were ever the same
till now. Encased in plush
Mabel's resting.

Snow's fallen on those fields she's seen
forever grazed or sown,
till new houses came.

Sunk in her chair she eyes the day
soon gone. *Don't get old!*
cries Mabel Verdun.

Comb the cold from her hair. She'll do.
Let her ride away in the sun
haycart-high.

Carry her down the lanes she knew,
call her tunes. Let her go.
She's singing now.

Karen Izod

Conscience

Presiding over the tea pot, Mrs Snowling
is careful to hold back any drip
for fear of the stain
on her daughter's white gloves.
Presented, back and front,
held out for the close inspection
of the Misses Lucy and Florence.

Theirs was a risky goodness,
a practical mission.
Refusing to condone
how a failure to take up arms
could enforce such solitude,
could crack the voice
of a preaching man.

And theirs was a belief
that knew how working this Suffolk land
could re-build a man, honour a conscience,
settle a country.

That evening as Mr Snowling invites a prayer,
a white feather falls through the letter box.
Snatched up, concealed in a spotless glove.

Note:
The Misses Lucy and Florence were Miss Lucy Taggart and Miss Florence Hill, both
of the London Postal Mission who provided small-holdings for conscientious objectors
in the Suffolk village of Bedfield.

Ian Higgins

French Poetry of the Great War

What follows is not so much an article as a selection of translated poems
and extracts from poems, with linking comments. This is because French
Great War poetry is very little known in Britain – and indeed in France,
even today. One could write at length about the canonic British poets of
the war with relatively little quotation, because we are familiar with their
work; but doing that for the French would be an empty exercise – dictating
to readers what to think about a body of work they have not read.

First, though, I should expand on the perhaps surprising statement that
French Great War poetry is still little known in France. Certainly, it has been
more written about over the last ten years. But even today, if you mention
war poetry to a French person the response is likely to be: 'Ah, les poètes de
la Résistance' – the Resistance poets of 1940–44. Why should this be? After
all, Resistance poetry was often attacked after the Liberation as mere verse,
reactionary in expression and content, not real poetry but propaganda. And
yet, for various reasons, a certain amount of Resistance poetry has survived
the onslaught, being studied in schools and, today, recognised as true poetry
worth reading in its own right.

The situation in 1918–19 was different. Much of the poetry published in
the war was jingoistic, technically retrograde, well-intentioned doggerel,
effective in maintaining civilian morale but unreadable nowadays except as
a historical document. So it attracted similar criticisms to those levelled at
Resistance poetry thirty years later. I shall largely ignore this verse, because
there is plenty of better poetry to look at – more than there is space for here,
unfortunately. Diction and quality aside, however, patriotism itself was very
unfashionable after the war in a cultural climate dominated by Surrealism.
True, Paul Eluard, who was to be one of the most prominent Surrealists,
never repudiated the poems he wrote at the front in 1916. Similarly, Aragon
published poems in 1919 about being under fire, and republished them
later. But during the twenties and thirties Surrealism as a whole rejected
war writing as a glorification of pernicious militarism. Even Apollinaire,
that most avant-garde of poets, lost favour in Surrealist eyes for having let
himself be led astray into writing war poetry.

While jingoistic doggerel was very prominent in Britain as well, the
British Great War poets we read today are less hostile to the Hun than to
war itself, or indeed to that very jingoism. So was there no anti-war poetry

in France? Of course there was. It could not be published during the war, except abroad, because of censorship; what did appear in periodicals in France was printed with blanks where the censor had ordered material to be removed. But then, even after the war, anti-war poetry was relatively ignored, as an insult to those whose sacrifice had in the end delivered France from the invader. And in that fact lies a clue to a crucial difference between French and British poetry of the war: deliverance from the invader was not an immediate concern for the British.

RH Mottram formulated this very clearly in 1927, in his novel *The Spanish Farm Trilogy, 1914–1918*: '[The British] had been welcomed as Allies, resented as intruders, but never had they become homogeneous with the soil and its natives, nor could they ever leave any everlasting mark on the body or spirit of the place.' As the following excerpt from Anna de Noailles' 'Verdun' suggests, French writers were acutely aware that the war was being fought on, and in, their native earth: 'Passer-by, think not to extol / The city hosts of angels shielded, sprung / From every inch of France's soil. So much blood / Has run [...] / Acknowledge, in the slashed and battered plain, / The fathomless and hallowed power of France, / Whose noblest hearts now lie buried in her soil. [...] / Soaked and sated, earth is made man.'

The soldier poets themselves often wrote of being part of this native earth, circulating through the trenches like the country's bloodstream. Apollinaire, for instance, was conscious of living deep in the body of France, as in 'War Wonder': 'I've gone flowing with my whole company through the war's soft sweet guts all along long saps / Flames keep shouting I'm here / I've dug the bed I'm flowing along branching into myriad little rivers going everywhere.' Lucien Rolmer wrote in a letter: 'I'm living like a root, and proud of it – I feel I'm steeped in French soil. I'm giving myself.' François Porché's 'Trench Poem' has a variant on the theme: the Germans in *their* trenches are 'Leaching through the soil like water from an impure spring, / Feeling for some narrow fissure / Through which to surge in one massive wave'. It was French farmland that was being churned and poisoned, French villages being reduced to rubble.

An additional factor was that France had been humiliated in the Franco-Prussian war of 1870–71. The popular revanchism that followed the defeat had largely subsided by 1910, kept alive mainly by right-wing nationalists; when mobilisation was declared, the predominant reaction was resignation. However, when Germany invaded Belgium and France, it was suddenly urgent not only to drive the invader from French soil, but also to avoid renewed dishonour. Small wonder, then, that even peaceable souls like Albert-Paul Granier, whose poem 'Hate', written at the outbreak of war,

160

ends 'Hate! Hate! How the words hurt! / Hate, we have to hate! / Hatred unto ecstasy', readily accepted the need to fight.

That said, there was in France, as in Britain, an outpouring of patriotic verse when war was declared. This excerpt from 'To Norman Lads', by Lucie Delarue-Mardrus, is a typical example:

Do you own, or simply work, the land?
– Arise and hurry! Now!
Stout of heart and firm of hand,
Save the fields you plough. [...]

Make haste! Sing as you depart,
And you arm for carnival;
March with poems in your heart,
And war is festival.

A great tragedy is about to play.
Leave no thing to chance:
Arise, my Normandy, away
And save the soil of France!

Delarue-Mardrus was to strike a different note in 1915: 'All Souls' Day, day of graveside prayer, / Bells tolling, guns' thunder rolling, / Our wearying hearts grown dull and numb / To bells, the alarms, and everywhere // Entire tragedies of lives undone. / [...] At last the bells pause for breath; / But not the drumming, willing guns: / While we are celebrating death, / The distance dins with killing, killing.'

There were, however, plenty of civilian poets who felt able, well into the war, to assure soldiers that martyrdom was exhilarating and beautiful if suffered in the defence of Christianity and civilisation against the Teutonic barbarian. By 1916, most soldiers seem to have found this repulsive, though they rarely swerved from acceptance that the fight was necessary. Early on, though, there were soldiers who themselves expressed such views. One such was Nicolas Beauduin. Before the war, Beauduin was an avant-garde poet excited by modern technology, who yearned to lose himself in a literally ecstatic transcendent new Humanity. At the outbreak of war, he abruptly switched to an archaic incantatory style, the new yearning being to sacrifice himself for a France chosen by God to save civilisation. 'Offering' is a good example:

I offer thee the life thou gavest me,
I offer thee my flesh that thou didst mould,
I offer thee, my country, my ardent soul;
Land of my birth, my blood be seed in thee.

May this, my body's fervent last oblation,
When this my sacrifice has fully bled,
Be pleasing to you, powers of salvation
Who guide the living and protect the dead.

This spirit of sacrifice must have reassured civilians back at home. Just as reassuring was the stereotype of the chirpy *poilu*, facing danger with wit and stoicism. Typical of the poetry conveying this are André Martel's *A Poilu's Poems*. Some of these are heavily rhetorical attacks on the Teuton; more are full of word play; many have a little twist at the end, a discreet reminder of the sombre truth. One such is 'Execution':

Itching all night long, it's never ended.
Stem the evil of the scratch:
In a shirt-seam, where they hatch,
One of the scoundrels is apprehended.

The time has come, let justice be enacted,
In all its rigour, with all speed:
Against such unrepentant greed
Humanity has suddenly reacted.

Louse, your bliss was brief as mayfly's breath –
The verdict's quick, no pity is expressed,
The perpetrator is condemned to death

And fingernail to fingernail is pressed.
A bit like us, as the war grinds on:
One sharp crack, you're gone.

The best-known French soldier poet is Guillaume Apollinaire, who carried his pre-war modernist innovations over into his war poetry and, from 1914, experimented with picture poems. For a good fifty years he was viewed with suspicion, because he often appeared to dwell on the strange beauties of war rather than its horror. The reaction is understandable: the fragmentary, vivid simultaneism of much of this poetry is so startling that readers perhaps saw it more as play than as nightmare. In any case, as scrutiny of the manuscripts shows, Apollinaire quite often deleted explicit criticism of the war, doubtless to ensure uncensored publication and to avoid demoralising his comrades-in-arms. Two poems, very different from one another, but equally typical, will serve to exemplify his war poetry. 'Earth-Ocean' combines word play with nightmarish vision. It seems to refer to a gas attack, the men's eyes streaming inside their masks, which have two round eyepieces and a big pendulous snout with a filter, like some weird octopus. The earth is described as a white sea, doubtless because Apollinaire was stationed in a region where the bedrock and soil are chalky.

> I've built a house out in mid-Ocean
> Its windows are the rivers running from my eyes
> Octopuses swarm all over the walls
> Hear their triple hearts beating and their beaks against the windows
> > House awash
> > House aflame
> > Time a-winging
> > Time a-singing
> > The planes are laying eggs
> > Watch out they're dropping anchor
> Watch out the dropping angry ink
> Were you but from heaven
> Heaven's honeysuckle climbs skyward
> Earth's octopuses palpitate
> And then so many of us so many busy digging our graves
> Pale octopuses of the chalky waves pale-beaked octopuses
> Around the house is this ocean that you know my friend
> And is never still

The very different 'Horseman's Farewell' is a notorious example of what for so long was taken to be Apollinaire's flippancy:

> God yes! war's a lovely thing
> With all the songs the lazy days
> How I've rubbed and buffed this ring
> I hear you sighing in the breeze
>
> God bless! there's the call to go
> He mounted turned off past the gate
> Arrived and died while she at home
> Sat smiling at the quirks of fate

The rigorously orthodox verse reflects the girl's perfect world: perhaps she has just got engaged. But her world is about to disintegrate, though she does not know it. Is Apollinaire *really* saying it's a lovely war? Georges Chennevière, an anti-militarist socialist who served in the infantry, certainly did not think it was, as these lines from 'Fresh Supplies' show: 'War's gone to ground / To chew away the very world's living flesh, / Its appetite and health both in the pink. / O War, from your armies, endlessly renewed / Like tribes of rats breeding in ships' bowels, / Gorge and swill, unheeding of tomorrow – / For you have rations here for months to come! // The universe watches us; washes its hands.'

No less aware than Chennevière of the universality of the tragedy, Marc de Larreguy de Civrieux nevertheless aimed particular scorn at the armchair generals in Paris, above all the right-wing nationalist Maurice Barrès, whose regular column in the *Echo de Paris* angered front-line soldiers with its sabre-rattling chauvinism. Here is Larreguy's 'Epistle from a Monkey in the Trenches to a Parrot in Paris':

Have you read the paper, little Jacko?
I seem to hear you jabbering away
    – In the comicallest way –
    With all the military rococo
    Of the headlines of the *Echo*:
'Crrr... Crrr... Over by Chrrristmas... The Hun must pay...'
    And planning orgies of brioches
    With flour milled from bones of Boches!
    So there you are, in parrotry
    Mirror to your Matamore
    (E'er the Captain of necrolatry)
    Who, far from eye of Goth and Thor,
    For simpleton lays down the law,
    And signs the column Monsieur... Braggartry!
    Believe you me, I'm proud to know
    So very clever a macaw,
    Who imitates his Master's crow
    And squawks: 'Stand fast!... Esprrrit de corps!'
    – We forest monkeys never show
    Ourselves to men, out in Argonne:
    We have forgotten man, and gone
    More savage than you've ever known!

'Will out in the flesh what's bred in the bone,'
   Any biped hack might echo:
To ape a man is to disgrace your own,
Unless you are a jingoist or Jacko.
So I'll just remain
          Yours faithfully
                Macaque.

Larreguy was killed at Verdun, aged 19. Not surprisingly, his poem, like Chennevière's, was not published until after the war.

Another soldier, Albert-Paul Granier, did publish an outstanding collection of war poems in 1917. Like Apollinaire, more often than moralising he tackles the 'aesthetic' side of war, expressing what threaten to be the inexpressible sensations of front-line experience. Granier wrote some vivid battle poems, but the horror emerges unbidden even from descriptions of waiting, as in this 'Nocturne', set in an observation post overlooking the Meuse:

The guns have fallen silent, gagged with fog,
in the winter's night that cancels space,
and a calm, full of menace
as the screech of owls over castle walls,
hangs in the many-hearted silence.

Sentries, peering out,
tense every muscle, edgily
awaiting the unexpected.

A thwack like wet cloth
sounds from the valley –
sudden muffled rifle-shots
unsure of guessed-at shadows
and the rustling emptiness.

Tonight
is like the nights in Breton legend
when hell-hag washerwomen
kneel invisible at riverside stones,
beating shrouds in the thick water.

Much of a soldier's time was indeed spent waiting. But this was even more true of civilians, especially women, who were in all significant ways socially subordinate to men. Of course, with the men gone, farmers' wives worked the farms, many women did factory work, and middle-class women often nursed for a while – but essentially their role was to *wait*, in anxiety, as in Henriette Charasson's poem to her missing brother:

Only for rare, short moments do I ever understand, at last, my dearest brother, that you are dead.

For me, you left months ago and I simply think you have been away too long,

And I live my life as if I were sure they are holding you there in their gloomy forests,

But I believe you will come back on the day when the bugles sound our victory.

And I wait for you, and wear no black veils, and when friends' eyes fill with pity, I am all stubborn poise.

And they wonder that I can be so brave – but where is the bravery, when I still believe you will come back to me,

When I believe that I shall see you walk back in one day through this old porch, in the pale blue uniform you wore when you left, that last evening?

Together, we had walked out along the path through the peaceful fields,

And you, as you often do, had your hand on my shoulder, gentle and protective.

And we walked along, as one, in perfect step, as night fell round us.

– And that evening, perhaps, more than ever, was when we felt our love's full force.

You left with a smile, and said to us all: 'Back soon!'

– So how should I think you will never come back, when every promise you ever made you have kept?

It would be the first time you had ever deceived me ...

– And how pointless loving you would be, and how paltry my love,

If it failed to bring you back to me, back from where they say you lie amongst the dead!

No one has shown me proof that you are amongst the dead,

And I can place no reliance on their flimsy affirmations.

And I sit waiting for you, for there must always be a woman to watch the night-light,

Lest the sick man think he is alone and the soul depart the body.

Can you perhaps, if you're still alive, can you perhaps sense the still, small flame

From across the ravaged provinces that lie between us?

Sleep, my silent one; and rest; have no fear for the light, it shan't go out;
I feel I shall wait for you, month in, month out, my whole life long;
When my hair is white, I shall still be hoping to see you walk back
in through this porch.
Only for rare, short moments can I ever, sometimes, understand that
you are dead.

The title of Cécile Périn's collection *Captive Women* is variously echoed
in many of her poems, as in this one: 'I always thought that, clasped in a
lover's arms, / Being weak was heaven-sent, / And that soft surrender to a
strong embrace / Embraced with equal strength. // But now I hate – how I
hate – my weakness. / I hate these feeble wrists / That used to stroke him,
smooth and sinuous / In their bangles and bracelets, // And this lissome,
living body, on a chain / At the doors of empty dwellings, / That curls up and
sleeps when cries of human pain / And anguish fill the heavens.'

Naturally, some women poets did express explicit opposition to the war,
as a creation of male-dominated political systems. They urged women not
to suffer passively, but to take the initiative and say no. This was hard to do,
because of censorship. The case of Henriette Sauret is a good example. Six
of her wartime poems were printed with great gaps in them, where the censor
had cut material. 'The Ladies' has 35 lines missing, practically half the poem:

Left at home are the baby-machines,
The breeders bred to perpetuate the race.
Their happiness dies when their lovers leave;
They meekly stay behind and know their place. […]

It's to protect their home and their hearth,
It's for them and their latest brat
That their sons and husbands charge to their death!

For them? So why, when the decisions are made,
Are their needs and wishes never weighed?
They're lucky they're allowed to suffer and fear:
Their share is waiting, and silence, and tears. […]

So here you stay, idle-handed, dutiful,
Noble Penelopes elegantly prinking –
Yes, you *are* still allowed to be beautiful,
And to read the papers, so you know what you're thinking,
And to show yourselves round hospital beds,

Or even dress up and be ambulance drivers –
You have to have contacts, of course, and not be low-bred,
Know the odd bishop, and be a good briber.

So here you are, manacled in pretty fripperies
That none of you can even feel. Flatteries
Flutter down around you from the skies –
You're bound, you're gagged, with treachery and lies!

The last 29 lines were censored...

What of the aftermath? When the armistice was signed, there were
naturally many poems marking the day, typically a mixture of rejoicing,
guilt at having survived, and desolation that the dead soldiers don't know
it's over. Subsequently, many poets commented bitterly on the waste, and
on the shabby treatment of disabled ex-servicemen. One such was Marcel
Sauvage, but his aftermath poems embraced a spread of themes; this one,
'Recall-up', is a post-war variant on the common wartime theme of the
inability of the civilian to understand the soldier's experience, and of the
soldier to express it:

Suppose, all at once,
Blood were to bead
From mahoganies
And walls and hangings
In your drawing-rooms?

Suppose, in the night, all at once
The lamps bled,
Lights like wounds?
Or your rugs swelled and
Blew open, like bellies of dead horses?

Suppose the violins
Took up
The tears of the men,
The last refrain of the men
With blown-open skulls across every plain on the globe?

Suppose your diamonds, your bright diamonds,
Now were only eyes
Madness-filled
All round you, in the night,
All at once?

What would you tell of life
To a skeleton, suddenly there,
Stock-still, bone-bare,
Its only mark
A military cross?

Anna de Noailles shall have the last word. The tragic universalising of the 'body and spirit' of France in 'Young Shades' is in perfect harmony with the work of all the poets introduced above:

Limpid Summer evening, swimming
With swallows twisting and swooping,
Tranquil landscape, horizon
Awash with sunshine, blue sky
Lit with yellow plums –
What have you done with all the faces?

The faces of the youthful dead
Dissolved in your fluidity?
The handsome dead, sprung
By the hair-fine triggers of Spring
And the switches and filaments of Summer
Up into the urgent spreading foliage
Of earth's eternity.

Nimble, scintillating sap
That Nature is built from,
What have you done with their dreams,
Lulled in your pulse, lulled in your breathing,
And fulfilled as dew
In the cool, reposing shade?
These dead are the very flesh of day,
They are the fruit, the vine, the wheat,
Their sacred bones, distilled and gathering
Through roots and stalks, now fill and consummate
The spotlessness of space.

But that sweet, terrible love
That all the universe shouts of,
The stir and jubilation of desire,
Arms opening to shuddering gasps,
The ecstasy of tears and fire,
Those high triumphant moments
That no other glory can touch,
When we are Destiny's match
And the spasms inside us
Are beating out a future –
Who shall restore all this to the countless dead?
Who shall restore it to you, poor shades,
In your numberless oneness
Pining in the skies of Summer nights?

Poems translated by Ian Higgins.

Karen Leeder

German Poetry of the First World War

German First World War poetry was born out of, and for the most part coincides with, the explosive avant-garde movement of Expressionism. It is perhaps for that reason that the best of it is formally much more radical than the English poetry of the same moment. The Expressionist decade in Germany, from 1910 onwards, saw a radical new programme in literature, painting and film: a new conception of art and a new conception of what art could do. The poetry was characterized by 'erruption, explosion, intensity' according to Kurt Pinthus, editor of the most influential anthology of the time *Menschheitsdämmerung* (Dawn/Dusk of Humanity) of 1920 and embraced a thrilling and precarious vision of destruction and renewal. This new turn saw art in revolt against authority, tearing away the crusts of civilisation, the grand narratives, to favour an eruption of inner essence, existential imperative. It is easy to see that for some the advent of War seemed at first to embody that vitalist revolt and to promise the destruction of a diseased civilisation. Poets were swept along by the heroic euphoria of the age amid the wave of intense patriotism unleashed by the declaration of war and mobilisation; and many welcomed the war as a cleansing force that might bring the potential for spiritual regeneration from within. But by the time they had experienced the brute reality of mechanised warfare the vision had changed: barbarous technology eclipsed the heroic and the war of attrition (*Materialschlacht* in German – literally 'material slaughter') left no room for the human. Many of the individual poets associated with the movement met an early death: Georg Heym (in a skating accident in 1912); Ernst Stadler, Georg Trakl and Alfred Lichtenstein in the opening months of the war; and August Stramm died in action 1915. Indeed the fates of the poets reflected the fate of the Expressionist movement itself which – by the time the famous anthology was published – was over. It is perhaps for this reason that, aside from one or two individual poems, this body of work is so little known in English.[1]

Despite the fact that the young Expressionist Georg Heym (1887-1912)

---

[1] In English see Patrick Bridgwater's excellent, *The German Poets of the First World War* (London and Sydney: Croom Helm, 1985) or the two volumes of the journal *Oxford German Studies*, *Expressionism I* (2012) and *Expressionism II* (2013), edited by Ritchie Robertson for an overview of the movement.

died at the age of 24, two years before the beginning of the war, his 'Der Krieg' ('The War') published in his collection *Umbra Vitae* (1912) is often considered the first German First World War poem. It opens with an image of a chthonic demon that has woken from slumber and risen from the depths. It stalks across an apocalyptic landscape (to a heavy 6-beat trochaic tread), stoking the fires with human bodies, and making civilisation tremble as fire and brimstone rain down on Gomorrah. With the outbreak of war this poem was invested with prophetic significance and became hugely influential. In the early days of hostilities in Germany some 50,000 poems were written daily about the War: many of them caught up in the jingoistic mood of the times. Several of the great poets of the day followed suit. The 'Fünf Gesänge. August 1914' ('Five Songs. August 1914') written by Rainer Maria Rilke (1875-1926) in the first days of war is in many ways a direct response to Heym. Once again the war appears as a risen God, thundering in a red sky, and engaged in some grim harvest: 'For the first time I see you rising, / hearsaid, remote, incredible War-God'. This figure derives from a heroic tradition and the diction is rhetorical, hymnic, reminiscent of the great poet Friedrich Hölderlin and founded on an understanding of the poet as visionary seer. Though the war and 1918 Revolution would afterwards drive Rilke into exile and a decade of existential crisis and silence, this sequence of poems bears little of a true apprehension of war. Stefan George (1868-1933), esoteric *Jugendstil* poet of the turn of the century, also felt compelled to address the subject of war. His 'Der Krieg' ('War') of 1915, though different in tone, also shared the prophetic quality, offering a monumentally impersonal vision of the grandeur of the destruction to come: 'The greater part was past and no one saw / The worst is yet to come, and no one sees'.

But it was the reality of war on the battlefields, the 'horrible beastliness of war' (Owen), that left its mark on those who saw active service. The impossibility of reconciling modern methods of war with traditional concepts of heroism is a theme that marks many poems. However, it was the Austrian non-combatant Karl Kraus (1874-1936) who put it most cogently in his vitriolic satire 'Der neue Krieg' ('Modern War'). 'In this war I find it most difficult to reconcile: / gas mask and pennon'. He coins the word 'chlorreich' to pun on 'Glor' (glory) and 'Chlor' (chlorine). Those dealing death with chemical means remain 'chloriously' at their posts. The glory of war is evacuated and the poems are committed not to the imperatives of heroic action, but to exposing the futility and the tragedy of the fighting.

On 1 August 1914 Alfred Lichtenstein (1889-1914) was about to finish his year of compulsory military service and, despite volunteering for service, like many of his compatriots had no enthusiasm for combat or the larger project of war. His 'Doch kommt ein Krieg' ('A War is on its Way', 9-10 July 1914) offers no vision of glory, no illusions, but an ironic understatement most reminiscent perhaps of Siegfried Sassoon:

You freeze in tents. You burn all over. You starve.
Drown. Get blown up. Bleed to death. Fields rattle their last.
Church towers topple. The horizons will be in flames.

Low-key poems, often without rhyme, offer real, unheroic observations – for the most part laced with a mordant humour that looks askance at the absurdity of it all. Lichtenstein was sent to the Western Front on 8 August, but before leaving (probably on that very day) he sent off the remarkable poem 'Abschied' ('Departure'). It was published the same year in a patriotic pamphlet, but that context signals a fatal misunderstanding of his tone. In a simple, colloquial language, a sequence of rhymed couplets, reminiscent of the great German ironist Heinrich Heine, he eschews all bombast to foresee the banality of his own death in a vision the more bleak for its offhand tone: 'In the sky the sunset is glowing red. / In thirteen days maybe I'll be dead'. In fact he would have forty-eight more days. His 'Gebet vor der Schlacht' ('Prayer before Battle'), written just before the first large-scale infantry engagement of the war on 14 August 1914, is a decidedly unheroic prayer to be sung *sotto voce* by the men of Lichtenstein's unit. It expresses not the desire for glory or heroism but the unapologetic will to survive: 'That I don't die like a dog / for the precious fatherland'. Mocking the common heroic form of the battle prayer, the lyric subject wants nothing more than to return home to milk cows, 'stuff girls', beat up the idiot Joe. He prays that one of his friends Meyer or Huber will take the fatal bullet in his place, and that he might be let off with a 'minor leg wound, a little arm injury' so that he can return home a 'hero' with tales to tell. In desiring a 'hero's return' he is satirising the much eulogised notion of the 'hero's death', but he is also restating the most basic premise of all: to survive is all. The honest realism of the poem is practically unheard of in the war poetry of this time.

The struggle to find a language and a form adequate to express the reality of the war led two of the most striking and original of German First World War poets in diametrically opposed directions. August Stramm (1874-1915) created a radically experimental diction characterised by extreme laconism and August Schnack (1892-1973) pioneered a vast collection of sonnets in which the extraordinary long lines constantly threaten to escape artistic control.

As an Army Reserve Stramm was called up immediately after the outbreak of war and saw action on the western Front, in Vosges and Alsace, the eastern Front, and in the Galician campaign in 1915 as a Battalion Commander. When he fell in Galicia on 1 September 1915 Alfred Döblin wrote a moving private tribute in which he remarked that 'no one was of such an advanced Expressionism'. Between Autumn 1914 and summer 1915 Stramm had written thirty-one 'war poems' (though the word 'war' appears only twice), which issued into the collection *Tropfblut* (*Dropblood*) published posthumously in 1919. In these poems extreme physical and psychological states are condensed into brutally truncated forms, in which vivid image-clusters, neologisms and linguistic dislocations invoke the sensations of the battlefield. Linguistic logic is destabilised, grammatical relations are challenged, and human agency is all but removed to create poems of acute and unadorned horror. Most striking is perhaps the refusal to lend any meaning to the experience of war. Instead, the poems aim to recreate in an unmediated way the reality of the actual experience. Stramm had written of feeling like one of the 'living dead', anchorless and evacuated, a 'hard-shelled empty nut'. His poems give something of the same sense. And yet at the same time his is a poetry of an extreme and overwrought sensitivity, where verbs take on threatening form as nouns, and violence seems to emerge from the very landscape without human agency. The feeling is a sense of constant external attack. The ten-line poem 'Sturmangriff' ('Assault' – literally 'storm attack', the technical term for the attack on a military position), for example, begins: 'From all corners shriek fears urgencies'. After a series of single syllable lines it concludes: 'The heavens shred. / Blindly the horror butchers about wildly'. Stramm's 'Patrouille' ('Patrol') deserves perhaps to be quoted in full.

Die Steine feinden
Fenster grinst Verrat
Äste würgen
Berge Sträucher blättern raschlig
Gellen
Tod

(The stones are hostile
Window grins treachery
Branches strangle
Mountains bushes brush off leaves rustling
Shrieking
Death)

The first line already introduces the strangeness: the stones seem animate and bristle with enmity: the verb 'feinden' is a neologism from 'anfeinden' (something like 'emnify') which is driven by the inner echo with 'Steine' (or stones) suggesting a world in league against the perceiving subject. A window (there is though no 'indefinite' or 'definite article') picks up again on the animated hostility. 'Berge' in the fourth line suggests first the plural noun 'mountains', but also the adjective 'mountainous' and could be read as a form of the verb 'bergen' to shelter. The shrieking (it could be read as 'to shriek') and the death of the final line stand alone without a subject; the whole poem without punctuation. Although spare, almost lapidary, it opens into infinite silence.

Unlike Stramm, Schnack was for a long time scarcely known even in Germany. He briefly served at the Somme and Verdun but after an accident was sent to recuperate and never returned to the front line. His collection *Tier rang gewaltig mit Tier* (*Animal Struggled mightily with Animal*) was published as a limited edition of 1000 copies in 1920 and consists of sixty huge sonnets spanning some eighty pages. Although his experience of the front was only brief, Schnack also drew on the many poems and reports he read, and offers powerful tableaux of the new warfare, the carnage of the mechanised combat and gas after 1916. The collection is a single almost narrative sequence which follows an apocalyptic journey, spliced with dreams and premonitions, in which ephemeral ghostly humans move through a blasted landscape and are overshadowed by vast skies of stars. Like Wilfred Owen, whom he could not have known at the time, Schnack wrote rhymed lines of varying length in free rhythms; like Owen he is concerned with 'whatever mourns in man / before the last sea and the hapless stars'. He couches his visions of death and darkness in sonnet form. Although this form was common during the war, Schnack's use of it was extraordinary: the lines so long that the rhymes are almost eclipsed and the sheer intensity of the language threatens to explode the form.

Many of the poems find their place in the trenches, the shell-craters or, as in 'Schreie' ('Screams'), the barbed wire. This harrowing poem accompanies a soldier as he dies painfully, out of reach, but within earshot, of his comrades: 'There were nights shattered with screams with great screams of death, coming brokenly from the bottom of men's hearts, demented and full of lament / Dark human sounds in which affliction sang, red and northern, screams in which seas roared and furious storms'. At the end of the poem, there is Schnack's characteristic move upwards above the traffic of human life: 'Stars hung silver among them, a white play of light. If a brow stood out it was soon shrouded in smoke and noise…'.

No discussion would be complete without mention of Georg Trakl (1887-

1914), perhaps the definitive voice of the First World War in German. He was an Austrian whose fragile psyche meant that in many ways the war was an extension of his haunted inner state. Amidst visions of chaos – in a letter of 1913 he had complained of 'things falling apart' – he wrote poems as a kind of redemptive prayer. At the outbreak of war Trakl volunteered for active service and was sent to Austrian-occupied Poland on 24 August, 1914. He was a medical orderly attached to a field hospital in Galicia near the town of Grodek, the scene of savage battles in August 1914. After he was left alone for two days in a barn with ninety severely wounded men and inadequate drugs to treat them, his mind turned and, having first tried to shoot himself, he died in hospital on 3 November as the result of an overdose of cocaine. Although many of his poems mourn the decline of the age and foresee the end of man as a spiritual being in a brutish future, he wrote only a handful of poems that could really be called war poems. In these his Nietzschean vision of disintegration is inflected by the reality of trench warfare.

Trakl's last poem 'Grodek' stands in an extraordinary way at the crossroads of his private poetic world and the reality of the public historical event. The first line seems to read as a conventionally melancholy autumn poem before pivoting on the line-break into a darker vision: 'In the evening the autumn woods resound / with deadly weapons' (a point intensified by the echo of 'tönen', to resound and 'tödlich', deadly). After that, the landscape of the poem is increasingly dislocated – a dislocation that carries over into the grammar – with the sun rolling 'more darkly' across the plains and truncated visions of human bodies identified only by their 'broken mouths', their wild lament. The language appears to operate under catastrophic pressure: images are run together in paratactic associations; colours seem to exist of their own accord: the red of clouds or gathering blood, the lunar coolness of the night sky. And there are ghostly reminiscences of heroic metres crumbling under the extremity of experience. Throughout, the poem is driven by the tension between chaos and order. But at the centre stands the line 'All roads lead to black corruption' (the only complete and straightforward sentence in the piece) which lifts as it were out of the immediate reality to a darker, more encompassing vision. And although the shadowy figure of a mythologised sister appears to greet the dead as the flutes of autumn sound, the poems finally turns in a larger despair to an unknown future and the unborn generations sacrificed at the brazen altars of war. Though largely dispensing with the particularity that poems of war depend on for their effect, or rather skewing that particularity through a unique and primal vision, Trakl's poems offer a haunting imprint of the reality of War.

It was only later, at the end of the war, when the patriotic, nationalistic and militaristic allegiances that had been largely unquestioned in 1914 were finally debunked, that the possibility emerged for epic or satirical treatment. Karl Kraus's 'Der neuer Krieg' (discussed above) could only be published at the end of the war; and an equally bitter anti-heroic ballad 'Der Sterbende Soldat' ('The Dying Soldier') appeared in 1919. Here in densely rhymed four-line strophes the dying solider stands up to the might of the war machine and refuses to 'die for the Kaiser'.

The young Bertolt Brecht (1898-1956), conscripted as a medical orderly in Munich in 1918 takes it one stage further. Having seen first-hand how soldiers were patched up and shipped back out to fight as soon as possible, Brecht's 'Legende vom toten Soldaten' ('Legend of the Dead Soldier') follows the fate of an infantryman already deceased. At the beginning of the poem, since the war shows no sign of ending, the solider gets the message and dies a hero's death. However, he is promptly dug up, pronounced medically fit by the doctors, cleaned to stop him stinking, fed with schnapps and marched through the streets to serve the Kaiser once again. The patriotic frenzy is such that no one even notices he is dead. Beneath the blood-spattered imperial flag and lost in the cheering crowds of Germans 'determined to do [their] duty as Germans always do', the solider finally 'goes off to a hero's death' for a second time in the red of dawn. This grotesque and exhilarating poem in which the ballad form is almost spat out in a violent doggerel with preposterous rhymes is one of the very last poems of the war. It is written, moreover, by a writer who would become one of the great poets of the Second World War and demonstrates how much had changed from the pre-war visions of a new and better society.

Poems translated by Karen Leeder

N. S. Thompson

Italian Poetry Of World War 1

On 20 February, 1909 the Parisian daily newspaper *Le Figaro* published the first Futurist Manifesto by the Italian poet Filippo Tommaso Marinetti. In it he proclaimed a new dawn in aesthetics for the new century, praising the virtues of the technological age, which he saw as a potential for spiritual renewal. It caused a sensation throughout Europe. Marinetti was perhaps a little late in his praise of machines, which had been around for well over a century, but it was the first time an aesthetic movement had lauded the speed, mobility and sheer power of the very latest in industrial innovations and proclaimed them almost as moral virtues to enhance the soul of man and save it from its comfortable bourgeois sloth. This idealism had a darker side. Marinetti also saw war as a source of renewal: *Noi vogliamo glorificare la guerra – sola igiene del mondo* (We want to glorify war – the only source of health in the world.)

In five years time the poet was able to see for himself what a healthy effect war had on the world. But Marinetti was an undaunted and enthusiastic combatant, twice decorated for bravery. Unfortunately, after the war his militarism and patriotism led him into Fascism. Indeed, he even joined the poet Gabriele D'Annunzio when he tried to rescue the city of Fiume (now Rijeka, Croatia) for Italy after the Paris Peace Talks had ceded it to Yugoslavia. Many Italians had gone to war against Austria-Hungary because of Habsburg rule over Italian speaking territories on the Adriatic coast, which they thought should be under Italian rule.

Marinetti's example was a model for many Italian combatants in World War 1, especially its poets, including an infantryman destined to become one of Italy's most celebrated 20th century poets, Giuseppe Ungaretti (see Ungaretti, special issue of *Agenda* Vol 8, No 2). Like Marinetti, Ungaretti had been born in Egypt, educated in French there, and was drawn to Paris as an artistic centre before the war broke out. This too was a familiar model for young Italian writers and artists who were ardent promoters of the latest French movements, most notably Cubism.

In Florence, Giuseppe Prezzolini had founded the cultural and political review *La Voce* (1909-1916) in order to disseminate the latest movements from Paris, although not – at first – the Futurism of Marinetti. He was greatly aided by the presence of Ardengo Soffici, a painter who had studied at the Florence Academy and who had returned from seven years in the French capital, where he had known all the latest figures from Picasso and Braque to Max Jacob and Guillaume Apollinaire. Soffici later joined with writer Giovanni Papini to found the more radical *Lacerba* (1913-1915) which was ultimately to champion Futurism, although it was wary of and contested the theatrical antics of Marinetti and his followers in Milan. It was this review that published many of the poets who then went to war, including the "Simultaneist" lyrics of Soffici himself.

This was the situation then in 1914. However, on the outbreak of war in Europe, Italy did not join the Triple Entente countries (Britain, France, Russia) against the Central Powers, despite considerable popular pressure to regain for Italy the so-called 'unredeemed' (*irredente*) territories on the Adriatic and north in Trentino and the Tyrol. These were granted Italy by the Treaty of London the following year, inducing it to declare war on Austro-Hungary and a wave of patriotic idealism swept many young men into combat.

Italy's struggle to regain the Adriatic and Trentino was arduous and bloody, especially in the Eastern Alps. Austro-Hungarian forces held the higher ground and for the Italians it was literally an uphill battle, that is, when movement was possible. The many fronts in this war (Asiago, Carso, Isonzo) saw the stalemate of trench warfare very much the same as in France and Flanders, with the exception that trenches in the mountains had to be hewn out of stone and ice and armaments hauled up by mule or manpower alone.

Nevertheless, despite the youthful idealism and the glorification of war seen in the early war poems of Marinetti and Corrado Govoni (who later repudiated his "Guerra!"), the poetry soon takes on the tragic caste of everyday survival in the face of industrial carnage, tempered with moments of bittersweet reflection on landscape, nature and comradeship. Although Marinetti had invented 'words in freedom' (*parole in libertà*) as the poetic vehicle for his message, the poetry selected here is much more imagist in tone, concentrating on particular moments and scenes, more often than not in the same kind of free verse adopted by the British and American 'Imagiste' followers of Ezra Pound. It is often elegiac and humanist in sentiment, but far more experimental in technique than British poetry of the Great War. It will subvert syntax, use surreal imagery and manipulate voice as some of the following poems show.

But the experience of war tempered many poets to react against avant-gardism. Some unfortunately embraced Fascism, where others followed the 'return to order' of the Neo-Classical movement that took place across Europe from the visual arts to music to poetry. (See the relevant individual biographies below for details.)

In all, Italian poetry of World War 1 is extremely wide ranging: from the typographical experiments of Marinetti and others to prose poems, dramatic experiments, dialect poems and popular songs and parodies. The selection offered here is taken from shorter works and showcases poets who may be less familiar than the famous names of Ungaretti, Umberto Saba and Eugenio Montale, the latter two also writing poetry during the war. The interested reader is directed to the excellent anthology *Le notte chiare erano tutte un'alba: Antologia dei poeti italiani nella Prima guerra mondiale* a cura di Andrea Cortellessa (Mondadori,1998) which gives details of first publication and first collections of the poems.

Giovanni Comisso *(1895-1969)*

Volunteering immediately after high school, he served as a communications officer during World War 1, then immediately joined the poet Gabriele D'Annunzio in the latter's famous irredentist occupation of Fiume (now Rijeka, Croatia) during 1919-21, to save it from being ceded to the new Yugoslavia. He then studied law, but very soon became a popular and prolific novelist, journalist and essayist. He wrote one novel based on his war experiences *Giorni di guerra* (1930) and published two collections of poetry, *Poesie* (1916) and *Bassa marea* (1946).

Resurrection

Trees husband themselves too honestly around cardboard villas on the hills. In the fields patches sprout with little feathers of grain. On the ground, light is reflected from the mirror of the sun in waves that break up on the last snows left on the mountains. The men nearby have ears of mother of pearl. A fanfare of brass, and the horses step to the music's pace as if carrying bareback riding girls over circus sand. A peak opens up in the distance, the air rings with the C note of the earth. The road gallops to my steps. Everywhere violets are born.

S. Giovanni di Manzano, spring 1917

Clemente Rebora *(1885-1957)*

Having studied for a degree in literature at the Accademia Scientifico-letterario in Milan, he became a teacher and began contributing poems to the leading Florentine literary journal *La Voce*. Having already done his national military service, he was called up as an infantry lieutenant at the outbreak of war and suffered a serious head injury from an Austrian shell. He spent the next three years in military hospitals recovering from the physical and psychological shock, but was able to resume his teaching career until a religious crisis in 1928. He destroyed all his books and papers in the following year and eventually took Holy Orders as a Rosminian priest. He continued writing poetry in a religious vein and two editions of his collected works *Le poesie (1913-1957)* were published in 1961 and 1994.

A Dead Sentry Speaks

There's a body turning to mush
With a crêped face, coming to light
Above the stench of the harrowed air.
It cheats the earth.
Although out of my mind, I cannot weep.
Perhaps someone can do it, or the mud.
But, man, if you return,
Do not speak of war
To those who do not know;
Do not speak of it where men
And life still understand it.
And if you can return,
Take hold of a woman
And one night, after being seized by kisses,
Whisper to her that nothing in the world
Can redeem what is lost
Here of us, the putrefying corpses.
Bring a lump to her throat so that it chokes her:
And if she loves you,
You will come to learn this
Later in life, or may be never.

Luciano Folgore *(1888-1966)*

While training to be an accountant, he became an early adherent of Futurism, adopting a Futuristic pseudonym (*folgore*=lightning bolt), and publishing hymns to the mechanisms, speed and geometry of the new century in *Il canto dei motori* (1912) and *Ponti sull'oceano* (1914), as well as contributing to the major literary journals. He served in the artillery in World War 1, then became a writer in many popular fields from theatre to humour, finally becoming a scriptwriter for children's radio and television.

Beyond The Embankment

Beyond the embankment, a dead man,
it could be anybody,
silent for ever; and around him
the music of things
starts to happen again:
insects buzzing,
rushes moving,
gas rattles and rifle shots.

Everything seems like summer,
life crouching in the sun
waiting for dusk.
Still many soldiers
in line behind the embankment.

Contemplation of the still air,
and within it the stillness
of appearances.
A silver spider's web
hanging on a dry twig
spies on
the insect curled up.
It leaves men thinking:
'Fancy death like that.
Poor luckless flies!'
And everyone looks calmly on
as if a stranger to the game.

Ardengo Soffici *(1879-1964)*

After studying painting at the Florence Academy, Soffici spent seven years in Paris (1900-1907), mixing with the artists and writers of the day, including Picasso, Braque and Apollinaire. Back in Florence, he worked first with *La Voce*, then with Giovanni Papini founded the influential avant-garde review *Lacerba* which, at first critical of Futurism, then came to embrace it, but with some reservations over the antics of Marinetti and Carlo Carrà.

Called up in 1915, Soffici served in the infantry and wrote about his experiences not only in his poetry, but in two memoirs *Kobilek* (1918) and *La ritirata del Friuli* (1919). From being a leading proponent of the avant-garde in both art and letters – producing the wonderfully titled collection of 'Simultaneist' poems of *Bif§zft18. Simultaneità. Chimismi lirici.* (1915) – he then became an adherent of Fascism and pursued a more traditional line in both landscape painting and metrical poetry.

On Kobilek

Fragments of shrapnel explode
above our heads
on Kobilek's white flank
near Bavterca

in puffs of smoke
white, pinkish, black,
that wave over Italy's new sky
like delightful flags.

A machine gun sings
in the neighbouring woods of fresh hazelnuts.
The bullets that graze our cheeks
have the sound of a long delicate kiss flying by.

Were it not for the appalling overwhelming stench
of these enemy corpses
we could light up our cigarettes and pipes
in this trench turning to mush in the sun

and, as soldiers more than brothers to each other,
calmly wait for death,
which perhaps will not dare to touch us,
young and good looking as we are.

Giovanni Vann'Antò *(1891-1960)*

Unlike his father and brothers who worked in the local asphalt mines in Ragusa (Sicily), Giovanni was able to receive a university education and, while having a profound interest in Sicilian popular culture, graduated with a thesis on *vers libre* (free verse) in 1914. He was thus receptive to Futurism, which he tried to introduce to Sicily with his own (short lived) literary journal, *La Balza*.

Like many other young Italians, he was influenced by patriotism to volunteer for active service against Austria-Hungary and served as an infantry lieutenant. He was wounded and on convalescence in Syracuse wrote a prose-poetry diary in French. At the end of the war, he lost interest in the avant-garde and turned to dialect poetry and the study of Sicilian culture. After many years as a schoolteacher he became a professor of Sicilian culture and language at the University of Messina.

In The Tomb Of Shadow

Calm peace silence
infinite spider's web
in the tomb of shadow

Unmoving
heavy enormous
I lie down sleep
in empty space

A little sad
I smile
like a good day
I open my eyelids

In the tomb
the sun
slips away
like a lizard

Giuseppe Ungaretti *(1888-1970)*

Born – like Marinetti – in Alexandria, Egypt, and educated in French there, he went to Paris in 1912 intending to study law at the Sorbonne. He met the leading French and Italian writers and painters in Paris and also the Florentine Futurists, who invited him to contribute to *Lacerba*. On the outbreak of war he moved to Milan and was drafted into the infantry as a private, fighting on the Austrian and later French fronts. The poetry he wrote in the trenches was first published as *Il porto sepolto* (1916) and later amplified in *Allegria di naufragi* in 1923. He went on to become one of Italy's most celebrated poets of the 20th century. His poetry is collected as *Vita d'un uomo*.

I Am A Creature

Like this rock
of San Michele
so cold
so hard
so dried up
so unyielding
so totally
lacking in human spirit
is this unseen cry of mine

You pay
for death
by living

Valloncello di Cima Quattro, August 5, 1916

Poems translated by N. S. Thompson

Belinda Cooke

'Roasting Nightingales': Nikolay Gumilyov, Invisible Poet Of Russia's Invisible War

...to locate the gap between the constructed narrative of history and the silences and disappearances buried beneath it.

Eavan Boland

After a chance meeting with the Symbolist poet Alexander Blok at Tsarskoye Selo train station in 1914, Nikolay Gumilyov said to his then wife Anna Akhmatova: 'Are they really going to send him to the front – it would be like roasting nightingales.' This comment both hints at the high status Russia assigns its poets and the intelligentsia's mixed attitudes to the forthcoming war. Throughout the *fin de siècle* and exponentially after the 1905 revolution, intellectuals had become increasingly alienated from the Romanov dynasty, agitating either for constitutional change or all-out revolution. Many of Russia's Silver Age poets such as Alexander Blok, Vladimir Mayakovsky, Osip Mandelstam and Boris Pasternak, did not enlist or had patrons who steered them to safe locations. The war was welcomed by some as a means of speeding up the end of autocracy, which it finally very effectively did. Gumilyov, however, signed up immediately and headed for the front where he was to fight bravely and win two George Crosses. Ironically he, rather than Blok, later became the 'roasted nightingale', executed by the Bolsheviks in 1921 during Lenin's Red Terror, a period of repression which was used to consolidate Bolshevik power. He subsequently remained unpublished and written out of Russian cultural history for sixty years. It took until 1986 for his work to be published – the first evidence of Gorbachev's *glasnost*.

And yet Gumilyov was just one among the estimated 1.2 to 2 million Russian dead airbrushed out of Soviet accounts of World War One. This is particularly shocking given the fact that Russia suffered the greatest combatant and overall losses of all countries in the conflict. The most blatant evidence of such airbrushing is the destruction of what was originally the revered Moscow City Fraternal Cemetery. Karen Petrone's *The Great War in Russian Memory* (2011) is a moving endorsement of Eavan Boland's distinction, cited above, between official records and the truth. Petrone's survey of Russian interwar discussion of World War One in the face of official suppression makes plain that Russians did not, in fact, forget their dead. This is exemplified clearly in what she tells us of the cemetery:

> Information about the destruction of the cemetery is shrouded in mystery. According to the testimony of some local residents, the All Russian War Cemetery was desecrated when "neighbouring urchins ... played football with skulls they dug up from the ground". The grave markers were supposedly destroyed in 1932 on Stalin's personal orders. In another account it was the building of the Moscow metro that precipitated the cemetery's destruction and afterwards the People's Commissariat of International Affairs (NKVD) used the sight to bury victims of Stalin's Purges. What is certain is that some time in the 1930s or 1940s the Church of the Transfiguration and all monuments and grave markers were demolished with the exception of one [a certain Aleksandrovich Shlikhter].

But a hundred years later all this is changing in Russia. The graveyards' destruction is now well-documented and on August 1, 2013 the Kremlin commemorated the outbreak of World War One for the first time instigating a competition for the creation of a monument to be unveiled on August 1, 2014 (one hundred years to the day after Germany declared war on Russia). The memorial site for this will be Poklonnaya Hill currently devoted solely to the war against Hitler. In 2013 the Moscow film festival also commemorated the war with a number of World War One Films, the most fascinating of which is the one based on the first of the Russian Women's Death Battalions, formed as a last ditch effort in 1917 to shame male battalions into fighting more bravely. The Bolsheviks also executed Maria Bochkareva, something of a Russian Joan of Arc and the brainchild of the first of these battalions, like Gumilyov, in 1920. This seems to have been the subsequent fate of many who fought in the war.

It is important though to avoid the black and white treatments of history that today's Russian government now acknowledges with regards to Soviet treatment of the war. Russia's intelligentsia and her poets did not immediately become disillusioned. Initially there was intense patriotism and individuals put aside their dislike for the Romanov dynasty. The Russians felt close to the Serbs who were fellow Slavs and shared the Orthodox religion. Unfortunately a catalogue of disasters soon quelled people's enthusiasm. At the Battle of Tannenberg (1916) over one and a half thousand Russian soldiers inadequately armed were mown down by superior German cannon leading their general to commit suicide. Many Russians were sent without any weapons at all. The Tsar's biggest mistake was taking over as the war's commander-in-chief, leaving the capital to the Tsarina Alexandra under the influence of the detested priest Rasputin who was seemingly able to cure her son's haemophilia. This all served the purpose of speeding up the arrival of the February and October Revolutions of 1917.

Various poets' involvement can be tracked against the before and after of the unravelling of such disasters. In the early days in the newly named Petrograd many were involved in war work or gave poetry readings in support of the war effort. The Stray Dog Cabaret was the main venue for such events. This included readings by Mayakovsky, Akhmatova and even Gumilyov when he was home on leave.

Let's consider first the two poets most commonly connected with the forthcoming revolution – Blok and Mayakovsky. Mayakovksy initially tried to join up but was seen as too much of a political risk. When he did finally get drafted, he realised he didn't want to go. He was eventually assigned to a draftsman's office producing war posters. He moved on from his rousing patriotic songs to antiwar poems in eager expectation of the revolution. His disillusionment with revolution was to come much later and led to his suicide in 1930 where his suicide note tells us how: 'I stepped on the throat of my own song'. Blok, a poet revered almost as much as Pushkin for the musicality of his poetry, quickly became disillusioned with both of these apocalyptic events. He was enlisted into the army but was located away from the front, leading him to make the following comment: 'It was mud and blood and boredom yet they call this the Great War.' Though he lived out his war days in anticipation of the downfall of the Romanovs and found a pretext to return to Petrograd when the revolution unfolded, he quickly lost faith in that also. His poems 'The Scythians' and 'The Twelve' capture the experience of being caught in the crossfire of these two events.

Osip Mandelstam awaited the downfall of the monarchy with certainty. He wasn't called up and moved to the Crimea in 1916. Pasternak's initial enthusiasm was quickly quelled when he gained an impression of what the horrors of the front were actually like. It should not be ignored also that there were other minor poets who were in the war and wrote war poetry.

And along with Russia's idolisation of its poets, there is also the unusual fact (particularly in comparison with Eavan Boland's experience of the Irish sidelining of women poets) that two of Russia's greatest poets are women. Marina Tsvetaeva did write a few war poems but the moment both of her greatest poetry and personal tragedy was to come later during the Civil War, a period of exile and final tragic return to Russia early on during World War Two. She, like Mayakovsky, was also to commit suicide, in Elabuga in 1941. Akhmatova, however, rightly famed for her role as public poet both of Stalin's purges and World War Two, also wrote World War One poetry. She was inextricably linked to Gumilyov because she was still married to him in 1914. Their treatment of war however, was markedly different: he glorified it while she spoke of its horrors.

The remainder of this essay is thus Gumilyov and Akhmatova's shared story, not only because of their marriage but most importantly because, in spite of their divorce and subsequent marriages, Akhmatova sustained a deep fidelity to his memory ensuring that he was not forgotten after his execution by the Bolsheviks. And all this was done with well-honed Russian skills at evading the government censorship.

When reading their poetry side by side, with regards to the war poetry, Othello's words of Desdemona': 'She loved me for the dangers I had passed and I loved her that she did pity them' seem to define their situation. This said, early impressions of Akhmatova's poetry suggest she is less of a public war poet, and more of a woman love poet enduring the cynical indifference of a negligent lover, namely Gumilyov. One of her most famous imagistic examples is the following where she contrasts her desperation with her husband's indifference via concise details: she 'ran downstairs, not touching the banisters,' while 'He smiled at me – oh so calmly, terribly – /and said: "Why don't you get out of the rain?" However we are lucky in being able to get a thorough, more complete picture of the relationship via the beautifully constructed collection of translations of Gumilyov in Richard McKane's *Gumilyov: The Pillar of Fire: Selected Poems*.

McKane himself has always been a key player both in the world of Russian and Turkish poetry as well as in his lifelong work as a translator for Victims of Torture and his voluntary work for PEN on behalf of imprisoned dissident writers. Given Gumilyov's low-key presence in comparison to the other writers discussed, this Anvil Survivors Press collection has not received the readership it deserves. Now, however, in this centenary year it may find its moment. Let us hope so, for this collection has everything: McKane's own delightful prose clarity and transparent diction, perfectly suited to both Akhmatova and Gumilyov's clear photographic style of writing; a thorough introduction and notes from the world-renowned Gumilyov scholar, Michael Basker; and finally, best of all, McKane has astutely included an appendix containing all of his earlier translations of Akhmatova poems written specifically to Gumilyov. The result is a powerful and poignant endorsement of Gumilyov's life and poetry.

All of Gumilyov's war poems come from his collection *Quiver*. 'Five-Foot Iambics' is a good opening poem to set the scene on why Gumilyov went to war – a love of adventure, already reflected in his many travel poems. These powerful driving lines, with their regular beat well conveyed by McKane effectively capture his delight in travel:

I remember a night like a black Naiad
on the sea under the sign of the Southern Cross.
I was sailing south: the blades of the propeller
powerfully tore into the mass of the powerful wave
and the darkness momentarily took away
the vessels we met which delighted our sight.

Yet he goes on with lines which also in a threatening yet understated way
suggest the apocalyptic events to follow:

I was young was hungry and confident
but the spirit of the earth was silent, arrogant
and the blinding dreams had died
as birds and flowers die.
Now my voice is slow and measured –
I know life was not a success, and you ...

From here the poem progresses to painfully, powerfully and plainly
capture the failed love for Akhmatova: 'I did not dare to kiss your hair / nor
even to squeeze your cold, slender hands' and from here a vivid capturing of
the moment of the onset of war, August 1914. Interestingly both Akhmatova
and Gumilyov write of the oppressive heat of that particular August:

That summer was full of storms,
great heat and unusually stifling,
so that it became dark immediately
and the heat would suddenly stop.

When he moves on to the war experience itself, as Basker also notes, his
poetry is more aligned to, say, Rupert Brooke than the more realistic anti-
war stance of Wilfred Owen:

In the roar of the crowd
in the uproar of the passing weapons,
in the incessant call of the military bugle
I suddenly heard the song of my fate
and I ran to where the people were running
obediently repeating: 'Amen, amen'.

The soldiers sang loudly and the words
were incomprehensible but the heart caught them:

'Quick! Forward! The grave is the grave!
The fresh grass will be our bed;
the green foliage – our canopy,
the archangels' power our ally.'

Increasingly this sense of death as a noble cause links to a developing religious belief as the call to fight – 'hears the voice of God in the alarum of battle / and calls its roads God sent'. In another war poem, 'The Advance', some of his lines were censored for commenting on the rations: 'we have not eaten for four days' but his sentiments remain with the nobility of the cause: 'we don't need earthly food / in this terrible and bright hour'. All his lines are a far cry from more earthy realistic accounts of trench warfare familiar to many English readers, but Gumilyov's personal bravery in the conflict is well documented as someone willing to put himself into the most dangerous situations, so his lines stem from direct experience though they read more like imagined heroism:

The weeks flooded with blood
are blinding and light,
the shrapnel bursts over me,
the sabres soar swifter than birds.

I shout and my wild voice
is bronze striking on bronze,
I, the bearer of a great thought,
cannot, cannot die.

His poem 'Sun of the Spirit' continues in the same vein with a passion for the glory of engaging in the battle:

How could we live before in peace
and not wait for joys and disasters,
not dream of the crimson sunset battle,
of the clamouring trumpet of victories?

It is only in the later collection *Bonfire* that we see a more realistic, down-to-earth account of death in the poem 'The Workman' who is 'still busy casting the bullet / that will part me from this earth'. There is in general a more realist tragic vein here in the futility of death in war:

And the Lord will pay me in full measure
for my brief bitter life.
This is what the short old man
in the light grey blouse has done.

When we come to look at McKane's selection of Akhmatova's poetry, after
a number of her personal love poems tracking their doomed relationship,
he includes Akhmatova's war poem 'That August', where she is capturing
their shared moment of the war that lies ahead. This is all conveyed with
a beautiful imagistic restraint sustaining both Gumilyov's idea of heroism
and the woman's role to somehow preserve the old life:

That August, like a yellow flame
bursting through the smoke,
that August rose above us
like a fiery seraph.

Into the city of sadness and anger,
from the quiet Karelian land
we two – the warrior and the maiden –
entered on a chill morning ...

My brother said to me:
'My days of glory have begun,
now you alone must preserve
our sadness and joy.'

It was as though he'd left
the keys of the manor to the housekeeper,
and the east wind glorified
the feather grasses of the steppe by the Volga.

1915

However, what is hauntingly moving in the Akhmatova selection are the
poems that she writes on his execution, including ones where dates are
concealed to put the censors off the track. 'The Cried-Out Autumn' is the
poem she wrote when she first heard of his death:

The cried-out Autumn, like a widow
wearing black, shrouds all hearts...
Running through her husband's words
she cannot stop sobbing.
It will be like this until the quietist snow
takes pity on the exhausted mourner...
The oblivion of pain and the oblivion of bliss:
to give one's life for this is no small thing.

15 September, 1921

She goes on to write 'Incantation' in 1936 published with the date 1935 to conceal its being written to coincide with what would have been Gumilyov's fiftieth birthday and then finally 'Willow' with its significant reference to 'brother' and numerous other Gumilyov allusions. She would go on to write her complex long poem 'Poem with a Hero' which as Basker notes conceals Gumilyov deep within its lines.

And by way of conclusion to Akhmatova and Gumilyov's shared story is her final lasting tribute to him when she makes a pilgrimage to the place of his death. She tells her friend Lydia Chukovskaya of her visit to the unmarked grave where the Bolsheviks shot him at dawn in the early hours on 25th August 1921:

I know about Kolya [Gumilyov]. They shot him near Berngardovka, along the Irininskya Road...I found out nine years later and went there. Groves, a small curved pine, next to another huge one, but with torn roots. This was the wall. The earth sank down, dropped, because they had not filled in the graves. Pits. Two fraternal pits for sixty people.

(Reeder, p. 45)

Gerard Smyth

Islandbridge

The river heron and the young canoeist rowing
past the picnic tables and war memorial
go by with the speed of those in a hurry.

In less than a moment they are gone
just like the men who wore grey beards when I was young,
stoic and silent when their wars were over,

their medals lost among the knick-knacks
of cottages on Long Lane
or sold to the moneylender who knew they'd never

be reclaimed or worn on Poppy Day.
Theirs was a new nation without a guiding star,
those men who lived on to know their day was gone

and in the dreams of afternoon sleep
feel again the itch of a Tommy's uniform
and the blast that threw them into the arms of mercy

when the big guns opened fire.

Golden Lane

Born beneath cathedral bells,
he heard their morning and evening *Pathetique*.
The cheerfulness of their clanging metals
came gusting to his doorstep.

The boy from Golden Lane
with an ear for melancholy.
The idol of Paris, Vienna, St Petersburg.
The pensive maker of the transcendent nocturne.

Moscow congratulated him
for his lullabies to soothe the nineteenth century.
Night after night the privileged and prosperous
came to hear and applaud

John Field who made piano-chords
sound like the rise and fall of breath,
who when he played seemed to bend
and whisper to his easeful melody.

War

In memory of Jack Smyth, Pimlico, Dublin

A child asked *What is war*
and the old soldier remembered
it is the place where men forget where they are,

it is night in the Dardanelles,
the generals at supper, the Tommy on watch:
a vigil-keeper holding his breath

in rain that comes one step after another.
It is advance and retreat on the roads of France,
courage to be with the dead,

the battle with no intermissions,
a dry-run drenched in the blood of sons,
the strong arm needed to carry the wounded

to the surgeon's table
that stands adjacent to the graveyard worms.
It is the curse on the map of Europe,

a country no one has heard of,
the big mistake of the fool
who thinks it can bring back peace.

It is what William Orpen saw,
                    sometimes through a soft blur.

Tony Curtis

One Hundred Words
from the Central Mental Hospital

I am here again this morning
talking, laughing, singing
with the patients: the lost, the hurt,
the just plain blown-to-bits sad.

A few miles away at Islandbridge
in the War Memorial Gardens,
a garden full of birdsong,
the Queen of England is laying a wreath

for forty-nine thousand five hundred
Irishmen who fell in the Great War:
young men who left the best
of themselves lying in the mud.

Sitting here amongst the patients,
I wonder how many lost their minds
in No-man's-land? How many are crossing it still?
From this crumbling trench I watch, pity their step.

Michael Mc Carthy

Tommy Spooney

We see him walking in the distance ahead of us
on the straight road towards Cullinagh bridge.
His black overcoat almost reaches the ground.
His white hair sprouts over the turned up collar.
His arms swing, his steps are short and quick.

When we ride past him in the horse and trap
he stands to attention and clicks his heels
and salutes my father, soldier to soldier.
My father does nothing, just cracks the whip.
The wars they fought were opposing wars.

Seven cows with their udders slack after milking
graze in the field on the hillside. Inside the ditch
there is no grazing, only rushes and bog cotton,
and thistles with red collars like altar boys at Mass.
The ditch is covered in stalks of fairy thimbles.

He doesn't live anywhere. Sometimes he sleeps
in a *bohán* surrounded by briars outside the town.
We see him receding in the distance behind us
as we rumble over the humped-back bridge.
There the horse decides to dump some dung.

The crows descend and start to pick at it.
When Tommy gets that far they'll scatter
and perch on a tree, waiting until he's gone.
He'll stop and smell the warm smell of dung.
As soon as he sets off they'll start up again.

The road now is wider than back then.
The hump on the bridge is long gone.
The river is dredged, the bog planted.
I see him there every time I pass.

Rainer Maria Rilke

Endymion

The hunt's still with him and the quarry breaks
    as through a thicket through his veins.
    Valleys occur and forest pools
reflect the doe pursued by the quick pulse

of that sound sleeper who's bewildered once
    again when bow and arrows blurred
    in dream dissolve so speedily.
The goddess though, young, never wed, the one

    who passes over every night
of time, replenishing herself, alone,
high in the skies, concerned with no-one, came

    down lightly to his languid side
    and as she leaned to look at him
his skin started to glimmer while he slept.

Translated by Harry Guest

John F. Deane

Strangers on the Earth

(Andrei Rublev)

Harvest festival, courgettes, and mackerel,
pumpkins, a bouquet of pompom dahlias;
plaques on the grey-nude walls, names

of the war-dead, rank and age, and no word
of their desperation. A frightening steep ladder
disappears into the loft of the tower; there will be

a bell, heavy and doleful, whose iron sound
will unsettle the planks you stand on, dust
disturbed; narrow slits in the louvred belfry walls

open – on one side, to a long neglected yard,
slabs at an angle, rust on the railings, the crosses
lichen-blanched and tilted; on the other – the living

town, roofs of the new hotels and shopping-malls,
bickering gulls, and on over the trees and fields
into distance. Up there, pigeons parade themselves

around the balustrade; when the brassy weathercock
skreeks to a change of wind, the ruffled birds lift off
into the most beautiful of arcs. The world awaits

some final victory, a flawless melody from the cracked
organ, watches for the three angels seated at a table,
with the chalice, an empty space, a gesture of invitation.

Merryn McCarthy

Le Poilu

[The French Soldier]

The chemin de ronde finds him
standing there larger than life,
at ease, arms drawn up as if to light
a cigarette. But from below he is young,
on guard, wielding a bayonet.

Lichen has clung to his greatcoat,
puttees, boots and breeches
since the now-lopped cypresses
concealed him. Neatly moustached,
reborn, he gazes across blurred lines

of valley mist to a cathedral
spot-lit like a target. So far south
what to him was the north with its trenches?
Less real than local history or legend
where Caesar's cohorts fought

the Gauls, or the Hundred Years War
against the English that saw his village castle
fortified. Heroic tales of the musketeers.
He watches now the seasons turn, harvesting
of sunflowers, vines, not men or horses,

though once German limousines slunk by
to rumour of resistance in the château.
For the Jewish girl peering through a window
he would be guardian angel
before the dreaded Gestapo.

Culled they were, his friends and he,
from hamlet, town and isolated métairie
to man the guns, go over the top
in unknown territory, the simple with the grand.
All French names then – Fourteau,

De Galard, Barrieu, Lamarque, Labattut –
some few survive. Only afterwards
an influx of Italians to run the farms
and cultivate the land, to court and marry
French girls, continue the generations.

Each Armistice day a small group
circles him with wreaths and readings,
a baleful litany. Children sing
the Marseillaise but fail to understand
his meaning, his silent rhetoric.

Olivia Walwyn

Chantepleure

Rain that sings

like gun shots in the dark

the tin tin tapping on your scalp
that's drifted up to take

the hits – the cold
metallic death dance

while you float

within the distance of a brain
only the rain that sings.

Tim Murdoch

Tercillat Memorial

This, locals say, is
the land of the forgotten,
too far from anywhere
to matter very much,
neglected by politicians,
seekers of self-importance
and revellers intent on
having a good time:

mile after green mile
of meadow and woodland,
leaf-camouflaged streams,
apples falling unattended:
just a few farms, hamlets,
an occasional town,
houses hunkered down
in secretive corners.

A friend to nature
in nature's steady care,
sensible to time as the
law of seasonal return,
you'll want to feel
this is the perfect spot
to live your life securely
according to long habit,

forgotten by experts
who plan the future,
rid of an over-eagerness
that follows the crowd...
Yet here in this village –
mere dung-crusted street,
a shop and a post-office –
this myth of remoteness

is negated by the words:
À NOS MORTS, 1914-1918,
and twenty-eight names
from Aimedieu to Rigeau,
called from their rest –
the silent, the dutiful –
the first summoned up
when Paris trembled.

Alain Fournier

Road-Song

'The Roads Untravelled'.
        Jules Laforgue

We had the fever,
        The marsh fever
As we went on our way,
And a warning the forests
Would offer only curséd sun

We had stories of broken stretches,
Lost irons, wounded horses
And crippled donkeys with broken hooves
Refusing to move

We had no memory
Of the events of the day,
Or any sense of arrival

Horses' tack and saddles
To make shoes,
Walking through rugged broom,
Our feet bleeding
And then drying out
In the dust;
        …We marched on,
Crushing and grinding
Heath and heather
For balsams
To heal our wounds

We could have sat in ditches
To rest our worn-out bodies,
We had no hope
        And nothing to say

We preferred disordered flights
On ravaged roads, the boundary stones
And marker posts
            Of defeated horizons
That we left behind in the dust
And met further on, always in the distance,
Towns with far away names
Sounding like the pebbles underneath our steps

We will never arrive at the
            City of Wonders
That is only a name and dead in the sun
We want to live in the
            Sun of Heaven,
Your skies, with our heads aglow
And ringed with glory,
Sparks for feet, and throats
Glittering in victory song, our songs libations

We had the fever,
            The marsh fever
As we went on our way,
A forest without shade,
Surrounded by the gaze of russet-coloured heathers,
Their wild fragrance within us.

Translated by Anthony Costello and Anita Marsh

Matthew Howard

Femur

La Boisselle, 1/6/08

Tommy bone or Bosche bone?
Held against my own, a short man's thigh bone
sheared below the hip; spiked scrap of bone,
blown bone; exhumed bone
lost from the rest, (killed twice); dumped bone.

Officer's bone or private's bone?
Killer's bone? Husband's or father's bone?
Salt of the earth or bastard's bone?
A dead mother's loved bone.
A picked-up-stick of bone

regimental never demobbed, bone
memory, bone immemorial, bone
utterly without irony, bone
without epiphany, bone,
only a short man's thigh bone.

A blackbird for Edward Thomas

The end should come in heavy and lasting rain –
but came instead through the falling tens of thousands,
snowflakes, out of season. As today this dropped
shell of a blackbird lays in my frost-rimed garden,
a stopped watch, irreparable as creased paper.

David Kerridge

Painting the Memorial

Hunched on the steps
of the granite workface
midway from where *Le Rallye*
faces *Les Mouettes,* he toils
to make wounds shine.

Thumbnail in rag, he roughs
at scuds of lichen, spits clean
the dusty stone then reaches to dip
into thick glass jars that huddle
apart, like lonesome tarts.

Mid-alphabet
his attentive attrition at scabs
skids in recognition; his brush
jerks epileptic, splashing havoc
in silver shards.

The painter's ministrations
have done his uncles proud. They glint
in the sun, switching on like mercury
signals: *Gustave* from the Marne,
Louis from Verdun.

Youngest of the trio, his grandad *Le Gall*
missed enlistment and the flu. A good
pair of hands but taciturn,
he'd panted the millennium out
in a survivors' home.

Furrows of silver
scintillate, each name and date
a codicil of outrage, a memory
of crepe. Bugles sound *le vin d'honneur*
the villagers muster, watchful, safe.

The Labouring Man

(in memory of Adèle and Albert Herter, parents of Everit – a volunteer in 1914, killed on 13 June 1918)

The labouring man
recoils
from the crimson swirls, the keening
where Everit had his hour.
Across the veranda, slews of rain
spatter among the slats
and gyring waves slap
onto the eastern beaches.
Ear to the conch,
he listens to the scrapes
of residues – cocaine-sugared
vin Mariani from his Paris days,
'the better to bleed,' he tries, fails
takes up his brush.

The labouring man,
kind ladies and sirs,
begs leave to spread his wares:
Adele, wedding-cake tinkerbell,
clasps her hands
in matronly witness, while
down the platform, Albert inclines
constrained to forbear
salon trash. Their faces stare
from the past to the future
before them, where Everit leads
the blue-grey scuffle of hoots
and tears while they, shifted
to the sidelines, dutifully play
their secondary parts.

The labouring man
is seized by a rush,
a lysergic displacement
clattering across the lens:
Adele is *Mutti zu Hause* pulling a thread
through Everit's eye,
the soldiers a charivari, their families
a grappling chorale
and himself a dancer of the Vitus
hornpipe, wet and electric
on the loveless sand.

Émile Verhaeren

From Les Ailes Rouges de la Guerre

Mourning

She had three sons. Boncelle undid them all.
I hear her soft voice speak, as shadows fall.
Long the red sunset in the woods has played,
Yet round her floats the mildness of the shade.

Though all her hours are hours of wretchedness,
She guards, for all her flesh's weariness,
A heart that treasures up this tragedy,
And tears that shine with its nobility.

I see her slowly plucking in the lane
Three flowers for her three dear fallen men:
My soul rejoices, as it surely would,
To see this grief go forth, a force for good.

Translated by Timothy Adès

Martin Burke

The Ieper Road

The road ended
In a shimmery haze

Curling to white mist
Over the neat cemeteries

Ieper: old roads and sentential trees
But new roads also

Leading us into
The declensions of history

Which I pronounced
As if it was a blessing

Gleaned from
The names of light

Where old roads and new roads
Narration and mist

Formed the substance
Of our longings

For the sunlit dialogues

Robert Smith

Scheveningen

after Max Beckmann

Side window, five a.m.,
the view, steeled for its dawn exposure
to his sleepless gaze: conservatories,
swept promenades, and bunting on the lawn
windless in the light

that, minutes from his own cities,
broadening across the tilted lip
of fields, their marked-out polders –
raft of a landscape sounding the drone
of its own lineaments –

fingers him here, on this coast
that heard the muffling of guns in Flanders
on a southerly, the sands unvisited,
the sea's plaintiveness creeping
greyer subsistences.

On a Sussex Landscape by Paul Nash

These hills
that gave so many
for the reckoning, the unfurled companies
emblazoned for France,

a snapping of standards
almost within earshot, cries brought back
to sound this emptiness and the vigil
of trees,

to be touched furtively
in the unwrapped silence of dawn,
the stone rolled away on a prospect
of downland,

that only the few
could witness, the air
too immense, eked out with the voices
of strangers

when in this row,
formed on a spur above Angmering,
hardwoods are stilled in their likenesses,
an unhealed sanctuary.

Martin Malone

Let Us Sleep Now

Vienna, 31/7/2014

Then you spot him after all these years,
on the U3 platform at the *Westbahnhof*
heading out towards Simmering.

You glimpse his profile in the tunnel's gloom
but can't quite root that lean face,
clean and good-looking and well again.

The long summer heatwave's been good to him,
tanning his skin caramel and free
of the pallor of your last strange meeting.

A tattooed bicep strains impressively
at the t-shirt, a booted calf flexes
and there stands he in his animal prime.

You smile with recognition, catch his eye;
not Saxon nor Prussian nor Pomeranian
just an Austrian boy heading west again,
not your way but up the line to Simmering.

Note: at the end of U-Bahn Line 3, Simmering is the location of one of the city's main
cemeteries.

Morgenstern

The East

One night, he thought to cross
the East over to the West
saying: What it will cost!
saying (with a big gesture):

Let us also, from behind,
cram silken hyacinths,
abundant carbuncle buttons
all over our bums!.
It behoves us not to bring
clocks only to intestines,
thinking of heart-stop
alone if savings flop.
Away with the entressed
privileges of the West!
Equality to each piece
all backs turned East!

Look: no tailor opines
on all this: A pity if…!
The off-cuts you've got
destroy the whole cloth …

a treasury of oriental texts,
wonderful, is wept over,
a 'last gasp' before the stuff
of customary usage is snuffed

Note: The 'he' who thought this up is no doubt the Archduke Franz Ferdinand.
Emperor of Austro-Hungary, whose armies destroyed the Ottoman Empire, and whose
assassination triggered the First World War.

Epitaph

Set up a plinth for me, friend,
all sugared in ocean depths.

A sweet sea of water, briefly me
after I am deceased;

long enough for fish in swathes
gulping me, to be amazed –

which, in Hamburg and in Bremen
means, the mouths are men's.

In your circles, I am forever
the well-wisher, whatever –

whether I am stone, pumice,
merely a bird plummeting

or even a man of standing,
the joke is on me, landing.

Translated by David Kuhrt

A note on Morgenstern's poetry

Terse, ironic, a devastating wit in his poetry, Morgenstern was angered by the hypocrisy dominating Europe prior to the outbreak of the First World War. He anticipates the modernity of T.S. Eliot and Joyce, but with no concession either to trends or to literary establishments. These were in the melting pot: there were none; although, as James Hawes points out with his penetrating account (in *Excavating Kafka*) of Kafka's rise to fame, if the cap fits, you wear it: ... 'friends in the right places come in very handy.'

In Morgenstern's case, truthfulness is the essence of the message he gets from the works of Friedrich Nietzsche and Rudolf Steiner (see *The Tension Between East and West*, 1927). With the demise of the Ottomans, Morgenstern sees an upheaval in old Europe without precedent since the Trojan War; the shibboleths of modernity had yet to be defined. His horizon was on the ground, not idealised in apocalypse or utopia. Today, having lost that middle ground, we flounder in the mud of a fashionable post-modernity, swallowing whatever celebrity offers. Asleep on an Unmade Bed, we queue for the Turner Prize to worship a pile of bricks. Future generations will gasp. Seeing how we cave in to conformity, Morgenstern, in his poem *The East* (translated here) puts his finger right on it. Nevertheless, he is best known for the humour of his 'nonsense' verse.

Regarding the matter of translation, if I am right in supposing that poetry, in whatever language, must flow if it is not to be prose, then the intended sense of a poem cannot be literal. I have therefore followed the sense of the originals in the two examples here, *as the English usage allows*, using an appropriate punctuation which differs from the German. Infelicities of this sort may be irritating to the academic nit-picker, but they are a necessary consequence of on attempt to capture in English the sense of the German. In the German (the achievement of Goethe notwithstanding), syntax and vernacular are toughly welded in a way that English can't manage, and the resonance of the German in Morgenstern's poetry is not easy to translate.

David Kuhrt

Gerrit Engelke

To the Soldiers of The Great War

In Memoriam August Deppe

Rise up! From ditches, mud-holes, rubble and concrete bunkers!
Rise up from carrion-stink, from chalk-dust and slime and embers!
Comrades, to me! Now from every front and field
The new day is coming, the red-letter day of the world!
Away with steel helmets and képis and deadly weapons of war!
Enough of bloodshed and enmity, let's honour murder no more!
I conjure you all, by your country's hamlets and streets
To trample and stamp out hatred's terrible seeds,
I conjure you by your love for a sister, a mother, a child,
For how else shall your war-scarred heart be to singing beguiled?
By your love for your wife – for I too have a woman I love!
By your love for your mother – my own mother gave me life!
By your love for your child – for I love them all, sweet dears!
And our homes are heavy with prayers and curses and tears!

Were you at Ypres the shattered? There too was I.
At Mihiel, the beset, the battered? So too was I.
At Dixmuide, the flooded? I lay there in front of you.
In Verdun's gullies of hell, in the smoke and the din, like you.
In the snow before Dünaburg, freezing and in distress,
On the Somme, the eater of corpses, I lay, just across,
Though you never knew, just across from you everywhere,
Foe to foe, man to man, body to body, close and warm, I was there.

I was a soldier and husband and dutiful, just like you,
Thirsting, sleepless and suffering, at my post or marching,
Hourly came Death to beset me, wrestling me, searing, screeching,
Hourly frantic I longed for my home, my birthplace, my darling,
Like you, and you, like each of you. –
Tear off your tunic! Uncover the vault of your breast!
I see your graze of '15, the scab and the bloody crust,
And there is the stitched-up slash from Tahure's infernal day –
But don't think I mock you, for I can reciprocate and repay:
I open my shirt: here still is the gaudy scar on my arm!

The brand-mark of battle! of shock, assault and alarm,
A sweet souvenir, long after the war is done.
But how proud we are of our wounds! You are proud of yours,
And yet no prouder than I am, of my scars!

You gave your blood good as mine, and strength as red,
And the same sand riddled with wounds drank the blood we bled! –
Did the vicious grenade's discharge strike down your brother?
Did your uncle fall, your cousin, your godfather?
Is your old father rough-buried in some hole?
And your jovial friend, your boon-companion from school? –
Hermann and Fritz, my cousins, were soaked in blood,
And my helpful fair-haired friend who was young and good.
His bed is still waiting in his modest room,
'16, '17, and his grief-grey mother, at home.
And where is his cross and his grave!

Ho! Frenchman, hailing from Brest, Bordeaux, Garonne,
Ukrainian, Cossack of Urals, Dniester and Don,
You Serbs and Austrians, Ottomans and Bulgars,
All doing and dying, caught up in the hurtling ruckus –
You, Briton from London, Manchester, York, Southampton,
Soldier and comrade, in truth a fine companion –
American out of the teeming States of freedom:
Cast aside special interest, trickery, jingoism!
You were an upright foe: become an upright friend.
Here is my hand: let hand on hand make a bond:
Honest and human may we henceforth be found.

The world is for all of you beautiful and grand!
With me, be amazed, after blood and battle have groaned,
How the green seas ever flow freely to the horizon,
How pure and bright all the evenings and mornings have risen,
How from the valleys the mountains upwards heave,
How round us a million beings thrill and thrive!
O, our highest good fortune of all is this: to live!

O may a brother once again answer to brother!
May East and West acknowledge their equal worth!
May joy shine again on the nations of the earth,
May men be moved to show kindness to one another!

From front to front, from field to field,
Let us sing the song, the red-letter day of the world!
Let every breast by this organ-voice be thrilled,
The psalm of peace, forgiveness and upraising!
And the searing, ocean-roaring song,
The tearing, brother-embracing
Unrestrained, with mercy gracing
Thousandfold Love ring out, till the earth is filled!

First Aeroplanes

From Les Ailes Rouges de la Guerre

Honey, colours, aromas of roses of summer:
Bright breeze's refrains.
But war sows the sky with the fearsome yammer
Of great aeroplanes.

They fly up so high and they thrum in the light
Yet we hear no sound
And their shadow stretching down from a height
Never reaches the ground.

With chassis outstretched, with curved rigid wing
They circle and prowl,
And wherever they go they hang threatening
With their evil patrol.

City people watching them scamper and wheel
Cannot even descry
On their leather flank or their nose of steel
An identity.

Though we shout, no-one knows who is riding unseen,
Or to what warlike ends
The luminous flight of the hellish machine
Inscrutably tends.

And all at once in broad daylight they've fled,
God knows by which way,
Making off with the city's terror and dread,
Their booty, their prey.

Translated by Timothy Adès

LA GRANDE GUERRE

UN DUEL DANS LES AIRS

Comment le sergent FRANTZ accompagné de son mécanicien le soldat QUENAULT, ont descendu un "Aviatik"

Anna Andreyevna Akhmatova

We had thought we were beggars,
with nothing at all,
but as loss followed loss
and each day
became a day of memorial,
we began to make songs
about the Lord's generosity
and our bygone wealth.

12 April, 1915

In Memory of Sergey Yesenin

There are such easy ways
to leave this life,
to burn to an end
without pain or thought,
but a Russian poet
has no such luck.
A bullet is more likely
to show his winged soul
the way to Heaven;
or else the shaggy paw
of voiceless terror will squeeze
the life out of his heart
as if it were a sponge.

1925

Translated by Robert Chandler

Sergey Alexandrovich Yesenin

Mist Climbs

Mist climbs from the lake.
Fields bare after harvest.
Beyond blue hills
the sun rolls to its rest.

Splintered, deep in ruts,
the weary road thinks
it cannot be long now
till grey-haired winter.

In the misty, resonant grove
I watched yesterday
as a bay moon, like a foal,
harnessed herself to our sleigh.

                                    1917

Translated by Robert Chandler

Farewell, my dear friend

Farewell, my dear friend, farewell –
        you're present in my heart.
We'll meet again, the stars foretell,
        though now we have to part.

Goodbye for now, goodbye, dear friend –
        no handshake, words or grief.
To die is nothing new – but then,
        what new is left in life?
                        27 December, 1925

Translated by Robert Chandler *and* Anthony Rudolf

Laozi

Firmly grounded

chapter 33

To understand others
is knowledge.
To understand yourself
is illumination.

To overcome others
demands strength.
To overcome yourself
demands more than strength.

Wealth is being content
with what you have.
This is true: though
a man may pursue

the paths of violence
to secure his own way,
only what is firmly
grounded can endure.

There's no other route
to longevity –
I tell you, you will not
be lost to death.

Tastes and sounds

chapter 35

My teacher holds firmly to the way.
She goes about her business
among the people, causing no harm.
All is peace, security, stillness.

Sounds of music, talk, food cooking –
passing strangers pause …
How different is the taste and sound
of the way: thin and flavourless.

Look for it – there's little to be seen.
Listen for it – there rises nothing
loud enough to detain you …
But if you use it, it's inexhaustible.

Translated by Martyn Crucefix

Martin Caseley

The war, the war

(part v of a sequence which appears in the online web supplement)

The war in the published memoir,
the war up on the screen,
the war that sleeps forever
in the fitful, waking dream.

The war of the stirring poster
and the white feather; grainy
Craiglockhart film of the limb,
fluttering forever.

The war of the trench exploding
into particles of earth;
the shrapnel of the modern world
slouching into birth.

The war in 1000 days,
the war of 'never again',
the war of the Pals' Battalions,
the war of the foxhunting men.

The war of the iron harvest
that still seems to be ours;
the war that will not let us rest
in the small, muttering hours.

The trench war, the war in the air,
the war to end all wars;
the 'over by Christmas' confidence,
the war of the good, brave cause.

That war they would not speak about;
the war we cannot stop thinking about.

Mac Donald Dixon

Wars are not Won by any Living Thing

Wars are not won by any living thing
The flailing and the blaring fuels myths;
Nothing absolves the carnage that they bring.

No heron rises on a broken wing
To hear dead men chanting from ancient scripts:
'Wars are not won by any living thing.'

Chorus of blight, resound your nervous ring,
Glorious deeds springing from swollen lips:
'Nothing absolves the carnage that they bring.'

Hymns whistle with wind on barbwire string,
Whines to the crack of automatic clips:
'Wars are not won by any living thing.'

Life's wasted youth still mourns with every spring
Of blight, their causes rotting with their blips:
'Nothing absolves the carnage that they bring.'

A puppeteer plays with his broken gifts,
And men like fools follow his wayward trips.
Wars are not won by any living thing
Nothing absolves the carnage that they bring.

Interview with Josephine Balmer on *The Word for Sorrow*

Josephine Balmer's collections and translations include *The Word for Sorrow* (Salt, 2009), *Chasing Catullus* (Bloodaxe, 2004), *Catullus: Poems of Love and Hate* (Bloodaxe, 2004), *Classical Women Poets* (Bloodaxe, 1996) and *Sappho: Poems & Fragments* (Bloodaxe, 1992). She has written widely on poetry and translation for publications such as the *Observer,* the *Independent on Sunday*, the *TLS* and the *New Statesman*, and currently the *Times*. Her study of classical translation and poetic versioning, *Piecing Together the Fragments,* was published by OUP in 2013.

PMcC: *The Word for Sorrow* intersperses your versions of Ovid's poems of exile, *Tristia*, with original poems tracing the history of the old second-hand dictionary being used to translate them. In particular it uncovers the story of the dictionary's original owner, 'Geoffrey', who, you discovered, had fought at Gallipoli during World War 1, near to Ovid's place of exile on the Black Sea.

In *The Word for Sorrow* you certainly offer a universal approach to war. Your parallel narratives from classical times and from the Gallipoli campaign of World War 1 indicate that hardship and fear are the same no matter what century. In both your arresting collections, *Chasing Catullus*, and *The Word for Sorrow*, it strikes me you are doing something new with translation, and indeed with poetry. I want to discuss with you how, as a classicist, you give old texts new resonance. For example, you say, in your prose book, *Piecing Together The Fragments*, that 'classical translation and creative writing have developed a close, almost co-dependent, relationship'.

JB: In that particular quote, I was thinking about the ways in which you *have* to be creative in order to translate many classical texts which are often at best unreliable and at worst fragmentary. And so, even in a 'straight' translation, there are always many creative leaps that have to be taken, creative decisions that have to be made. For this reason, classical translation can lead on quite naturally, as I myself found, to poetic creativity. However, it is also the case that the great, archetypal works of classical literature have become, over the centuries, foundation texts for all poets. This is not a new process, in fact it begins in the ancient world itself, with Catullus' translation of what we know as Sappho fragment 31 and continues in English (and Scots!) through Gavin Douglas to Golding, Chapman, Dryden, Pope and on to Pound, Logue, Hughes and beyond.

As such, it's a very humbling tradition but I see my task as a joint one; I use my classicist's training to study the texts very closely, reading commentaries and apparatus, so that I am immersed in the scholarship. At the same time I am also responding to those texts as creative stimuli, much in the same way that one might respond to a landscape, an emotion, a life event. As the distinguished Greek poet and translator Nasos Vayenas argues, a foreign text is raw material for a poet, just as any other. And so, in all classical versioning, such stimuli often overlap.

PMcC: Hasn't this always been the case, though, that the sensitive translator makes a different poem his own, from a given poem in another language?

JB: Definitely. I think the difference is that, with classical texts, you are working with long-dead languages from long lost worlds. Even if you are lucky enough to have a complete text, you often know very little of the context in which it was written. More to the point, unlike a translator of contemporary poetry, you have no author to ask or archive of papers and letters to consult for advice on cultural references or, say, the importance of autobiographical events, and so on. For example, when I was working on Ovid's *Tristia* for *The Word for Sorrow*, I soon discovered that it was not clear why Ovid had been sent into exile to the Black Sea from Rome. In fact, if some scholars are to be believed, it is not even certain whether he was exiled at all, rendering the poems some sort of huge ancient literary hoax. In a way, though, this also gives you freedom as it makes it entirely the translator's call how to pitch the tone of the work; is it elegiac or is it sardonic? Or both?

PMcC: I like the way you summarise parts of Ovid's *Tristia*. Sometimes you use your own translation of the classical text as a palimpsest, injecting your own images on top. How did you choose which lines of Ovid's to use and then juxtapose them with your own? You also talk about the 'blurring of boundaries'. Do you think, then, that there is no limit to the 'blurring' in classical translation.

JB: What I wanted was for all the different poems and their various strands to bleed in to each other to form an overall narrative arc. For this reason, as you rightly point out, I cherry picked the passages I used from *Tristia*, and sometimes changed the order of the originals so that the poems could 'speak' to each other. I wanted the last line of one to ask or answer questions of the first line of the next, whether Ovid's Latin text, poems based around Geoffrey's experiences in Gallipoli or my own experiences of uncovering/ translating both. In this way narrative boundaries could become indistinct, as could the perceived differences between 'original' and 'translated' poetry.

As for limits on this, it's a question I am often asked and I think the answer lies in the frame of the work; classical versioning in a poetry volume is clearly a different matter to that in a 'Black' Penguin translation. However, it should also be said that many of the latter can have less clearly defined demarcation lines than we might imagine, for example the use of prose to translate verse as in E.V. Rieu's *Iliad* and *Odyssey*.

PMcC: I like the way you use, in both your recent poetry collections, translation and the original to spark off each other. In *The Word for Sorrow*, for example, you have three personae, Naso (Ovid), Geoffrey (who is everyman), and the narrator (yourself). Does Ovid leak into all three of these, consciously or unconsciously?

JB: Oh, that's a fascinating question. Yes, he was in fact very hard to shake off... As I explain in the preface to *The Word for Sorrow*, I had come to *Tristia* as an exilic poem, a wail of grief for Ovid's lost life in Rome, seeing in it an echo of the hardships and deprivations of the British soldiers sent to fight this hopeless, futile campaign at Gallipoli. But the more I read the scholarship – and the poems themselves – the more I realised that Ovid's was a far more complex work than that. When I first read the view that Ovid's account of his exile might be a joke, I panicked slightly as at first such playfulness did not seem to fit in at all with the Gallipoli poems I was writing. It's not a view, I should add, that many classicists take too seriously but it does underline the tricky, ironic edge of Ovid's verse. But I soon realised that this was precisely what was needed for my poems based on the Gallipoli campaign; many of the war letters and diaries I had researched displayed a jaunty, 'mustn't grumble' attitude. And so, in poems such as 'Between the Lines' or 'Welcome Note', which explicitly use first hand source material, Ovid's ghost, sitting at my shoulder, whispering his teasing jokes in my ear, proved very helpful.

PMcC: You say somewhere that some readers want to know the demarcation lines. I have to say, out of deep interest, I did find myself wondering about this. Where do you stand on this?

JB: Well, I am the sort of reader who always wants prefaces, notes, appendices and so. On the other hand, I sometimes feel readers – and I include myself in this – can get too anxious about whether we know all the references or not which, in a good poem, should not really matter. For example, I wonder if Cavafy's historical poems have slightly dropped out of fashion compared to his more erotic, personal ones because readers feel they should know who all the very obscure characters are, although, to be frank, ancient historians would often be hard pushed to place half of them, while many are Cavafy's own fictional inventions.

At the same time, in the poetry world, too much explication is often seen as distracting from the mysterious, almost shamanistic, act of poetic creation. And it is of course the case that many readers do not like being told what to think. Mostly, though, I find people are fascinated by where quotes, echoes, source texts and so on come from – and, as a scholar, it would seem almost a criminal act not to reference them. In addition, the work of Anne Carson has, I feel, changed the ball game in that she includes scholarly essays in her poetry collections, as if they were creative works – which, of course, they are. So maybe the radical way forward is more notes, more talk...

PMcC: Linking back to my previous question, it was only when I read the Notes to *The Word for Sorrow* that I realised that you had used previously unknown letters you had researched – of several soldiers in the same regiment as Geoffrey. This makes his experience authentic, and turns him, of course, into an Everyman. Do you think there is a danger, otherwise, for a poet who has not experienced, say, World War 1, in writing inauthentically about all the blood and guts?

JB: Possibly so. Research is so important here. And we are very lucky in the amount of original source material we can all access. But then poetic empathy is also crucial in order to make those experiences highly vivid and believable, as in your own war poems.

PMcC: Well, I aimed at poems that just glanced off the Great War, no direct hits.

You are very clever at working with parallels, and at pattern. Did you think there could be a danger in having two different parallel experiences of war (Ovid's and Geoffrey's of World War 1) in one text?

JB: I was very aware of that. In fact at one point I was wondering whether to take the Ovid versions out of the book in case it was just all too confusing. But a poet friend, Cliff Ashcroft, talked me back in to it, his view being that this juxtaposition between ancient and modern was what made the volume different and original. It is, as you pointed out earlier, very hard to write about such huge conflicts as World War I, especially as its poetry is so well-known and loved, so much part of our collective consciousness now. So I saw these parallels as a new way to approach perhaps well-trodden ground and, at the same time, to underscore the universality of that pain and hardship of separation, from loved ones, homeland and so on.

PMcC: You mention also in *Piecing Together The Fragments* about a woman tackling male epics and changing them into female experience. What is your take on this?

JB: I think it is a very fertile area. Without access to a classical education, women have often been excluded from the study and indeed even the reading of classic epic. And translation is above all an act of reading as well as writing. But there do seem to be some texts more than others which women themselves have tended to avoid. For example, when I translated Catullus I was the only woman to have taken on all of his shorter poems (classicist Edith Hall later wrote that, as a woman, it was the only translation of his often very alpha-male poems she could stand to read). I don't believe there has yet been a woman translator of Homer's complete epics, although the American translator Sarah Ruden has produced a wonderful version of *Homeric Hymns* and also of Virgil's *Aeneid*. Versioning, too, has often been far more a male prerogative, although works like Alice Oswald's *Memorial* and Clare Pollard's *Ovid's Heroines* are starting to redress the balance at last.

What I do think is important here is that women don't just produce poems which tell Penelope's side of the *Odyssey* or Dido's take on Aeneas, fascinating though these are (and I've written plenty myself) but also engage with the male warrior world, subverting it, transgressing it, offering new readings which can perhaps only have emanated from a woman's point of view.

PMcC: It seems to me, though, that there is no such demarcation in your own work. You are one of those rare species who writes androgynously, someone Virginia Woolf would applaud. Didn't she say somewhere in 'A Room of One's Own' that there would never be a woman Shakespeare until a woman could write androgynously – like you?

JB: Well, obviously I would demur to Shakespeare – and Virginia Woolf – but it's an interesting view! Thematically, I would see myself very much as a gynocentric writer in that much of my work has been about the excavation and recovery of forgotten women poets. In addition, I have often written poems such as 'Feminine Ending' or 'Niobe' in *Chasing Catullus*, that give voice to the usually silent woman's point of view. And I worked hard to give my translations of Catullus a slightly subversive female taint. That said, apart from myself, the main narrative protagonists in *The Word for Sorrow* are all male. But I think here you are talking about stylistics, in which case

234

any sense of being androgynous might well come from the classical, in the broadest sense of the word, an emphasis on clarity and lack of adornment.

PMcC: It seems to be a fashion these days for established poets to broaden their scope and confirm their position in the canon to translate, or write versions, of classical texts. I am thinking of Heaney, Ted Hughes, Christopher Logue, Tony Harrison, Simon Armitage, Michael Longley, Alice Oswald, Anne Carson, Clare Pollard and so on. Can you comment on this?

JB: It is an exciting time for classics. When I first started writing in the early 1980s, there was very little general interest in classical texts, especially as Pound was very out of fashion (although *Agenda*, as ever, still carried the torch for classical translation and versioning which is why it is such a pleasure to be interviewed here). Then Christopher Logue published *War Music* in 1981, which reissued some of his earlier versions of the *Iliad,* and which just grew and grew in stature. This was followed by Michael Longley's inspirational *Gorse Fires* in 1991, containing versions of extracts from the *Odyssey*. Michael Hofmann and James Lasdun's *After Ovid* project in 1994 was also hugely influential, in fact it kick started Ted Hughes' writing of *Tales from Ovid.*

The translation scholar and writer Susan Bassnett argues that this explosion of classical versions might be due to the fact that the Bible is less and less an anchor text for our society and that Homeric epic, in particular, has taken its place. I think there are social reasons too; many of these poets are products of a new generation, often working class, who had access to classics via grammar schools for the first time and so later wanted to be inclusive rather than exclusive about this new world. Edith Hall sees Tony Harrison, for example, as looking to create public poetry with his classical translations and versions rather than some sort of exclusive curriculum.

I think these writers, in turn, have influenced a younger generation of poets such as Simon Armitage or Clare Pollard, who have suffered from the decline of classics in state schools and so did not have the opportunity to learn Greek or Latin, yet are still attracted to the possibilities the texts offer. I suppose I was somehow squeezed in the middle between the two, among the last state school students being taught Greek, even if it was scrunched up into a book cupboard somewhere with just two or three of us and a teacher, especially if you were at a girls' school (and even then I had to go over the road to the Boys' Grammar School to study for Greek A Level).

PMcC: Few of the above poets seem to push 'translation' as far as you do, though. They seem to produce more usual 'versions' of the original text.

JB: Well some do, some don't! Christopher Logue is very radical and much of Anne Carson's work can be very challenging... And Michael Longley has an exquisite way of moving from the ancient to the modern, and back again, in a single, often very short poem. Ironically, my rule of thumb is that the more immersed a poet is in the classics, the more confidence they will probably have to be subversive rather than faithful, a tradition which goes right back to Ben Jonson and John Dryden – although Christopher Logue, who knew no Greek, would have to be the exception that proves the rule. For my own part, I think one of the differences is that, with *The Word for Sorrow* and also my current project, *The Paths of Survival*, I am looking to establish a book-long dialogue between translation and original poem, a cohesive whole.

PMcC: You cite Pound as a particularly strong, liberating influence in your work. Can you comment on this?

JB: For myself, this influence was mostly in the arena of translating fragments which Pound approached with clarity and confidence, unafraid to leave them mysterious and broken rather than to fill in the gaps. I was also very taken with J.P. Sullivan's edition and commentary on Pound's often overlooked *Homage to Sextus Propertius*, which is an incredibly vital work, slated in its day by academia, yet shows the way to transform and transgress classical texts while still allowing them to retain their own ancient integrity.

PMcC: I like the word some used for Pound's translations of the Chinese Classics: 'translucencies'. Does this have any resonance with you?

JB: I think it's about delicacy of touch, about reimagining the original while still letting it shimmer through the new translated text. A palimpsest, as you say.

PMcC: Now onto the actual writing of your *The Word for Sorrow*. It must have involved a huge amount of research, and you seem adept at fitting all the pieces together like a smooth jigsaw. Do you enjoy this part of the process?

JB: Very much so. I love a good root around in dictionaries, commentaries, and especially being nose-deep in a pile of academic journals. It helps to ease you in to the work but at the same time I find this is very often where the light bulb moments of creativity happen. I have a big notebook where I write out the texts on one side, with two lines blank in between to note down vocabulary and ideas for the translation itself. I then leave the other side of the page blank for more expansive ideas and thoughts.

PMcC: That sounds very organised.

A lot of uncanny coincidences seem to have been involved in the creating of the book. In his book, *The Roots of Coincidence*, Arthur Koestler suggests that some of these 'coincidences' are more than random chances, linked to seriality and the psychic. What do you think? And can you elaborate on the coincidences?

JB: That's another very interesting question. In many ways, I think there are no 'coincidences', in that the mind itself makes those links, joins up its own dots. Again, it is part of all of our creative processes, in life as well as literature. When I was recounting the story of how I discovered the name of my dictionary's owner at a classics conference in Oxford, the Ovid scholar Jennifer Ingleheart later pointed out, light-heartedly, that it was very (and perhaps suspiciously!) Ovidian in its coincidences. And, of course, she was right that, in order to be succinct – and to tell a better tale - I had conflated several events down into one. So poetic licence also plays its part...

PMcC: Now down to the big question of 'saying the unsayable'. I would have thought this is what poetry can brave, and the 'unsayable', if deeply lived, becomes universal. We all react differently, however, to personal loss and trauma. You seem to need a 'place to hide' and to find a mask through, as you say, 'the prism of classical literature'. I know *Chasing Catullus* was inspired by the very traumatic loss of your young niece. Would you say this is very English: to avoid raw pain and transfuse it elsewhere?

JB: Possibly, yes. It is certainly very British to keep things understated. But here I wasn't so much avoiding pain as finding a way to write that wasn't, as I think Simon Armitage once put it, a blooded arm torn off and sent through the post to an editor. Yet, as I explain in *Piecing Together the Fragments*, this was also not primarily my pain, my grief, but my sister's, and that consideration played a huge part too. When my niece Rachel was ill and dying, I had kept a diary and had written poems that recorded events very much as they happened but I didn't want my family, particularly my sister, to have to relive it in that way. I also thought about the general reader; how much reality do they really want to bear? This was an awful, awful death of a very young child from aggressive neuroblastoma, visceral, disgusting, attacking all of her central organs, and it was not something everyone might want to have to face – or read about – full on. And it is the task of all art to transform such raw experience, to transcend the personal in whatever ways might be available.

More pertinently, by then I had long been working on classical texts as a translator and so classical literature and myth had become the vocabulary with which and through which I spoke; even when I started off with the intention of writing a 'straightforward' poem, whether of mourning or joy, in the process I was so often taken back again and again to the archetypes and classical voices I knew so well.

PMcC: There happen to be many very moving 'raw' elegaic poetry collections out at the moment, such as Rebecca Goss's *Her Birth* (Carcanet), and Imraz Dharker's *Over the Moon* (Bloodaxe), also Stuart Medland's *Last Man Standing* (Agenda Editions). In Michael Longley's new collection, *The Stairwell,* he mourns the death of his twin brother in a sequence of poems with many written in a direct fashion, rather than based on classical texts. This leads me to ask: do you ever write 'raw' poems, with only the white blank page before you?

JB: Those are all amazing and awe-inspiring volumes. And, yes, many of the poems in both of my books are also more straightforward elegies. In *Chasing Catullus*, for example, there are several poems in the sequence which aren't written through the mask of classical versioning, such as 'In Coventry' or 'Titan Arum'. And the same goes for most of the poems written in my own voice in *The Word for Sorrow*. At present I am also working on a sequence of mourning sonnets for my mother, of which half are based on classical texts and half are what we could call 'blank page' poems.

But I think there are two points to make here. Firstly, in many ways no poem exists on its own. As many translator/poets have long suggested, practically everything we create is, in one way or another, written out of another text. As Octavio Paz argues, every original poem is a translation. Secondly, we might equally also argue that every translation is an original; that we still face the blank page every time we sit down to work on a source text, to make it our own. In fact, the endless search for equivalence and perfection, where often none can ever exist, might create even more of a block than writing an original poem. So, as Nasos Vayenas points out, the process of translation is itself a poetic act. Certainly translation and versioning is one of the most time consuming tasks I know. It eats the days...

PMcC: You talk of the risk of being seen as 'plundering Ovid like a grave-robber'. Doesn't all translation thieve from the original in some way? Yet it makes accessible a whole body of poetry that could not be understood, in general, in its original language. Do you feel the use of frames, threads, palimpsests are props that enable the translator/version maker to be freed from 'the unnecessary tangle with the original'.

JB: Yes, absolutely. I think often the challenge is to make the reader understand that this is how it works; that you do not somehow press a translation button and one parallel poem magically reappears in another language. So being visible rather than invisible as a translator through many of the means you mention is hugely important. You are also right that sometimes it is hard to free yourself from the enthralment of the original; as Paz said so incisively, translation is an act of love and from this comes the desire for participation. But translations that are too respectful, too polite, can make the worst versions.

PMcC: Let us conclude, then, with Charles Tomlinson's definition of translation as 'metamorphosis'. And quote from the final two stanzas of your resonant concluding title poem in *The Word For Sorrow*:

> We none of us need a dictionary
> to define the word for sorrow...
>
> What drives us on, keeps us to our path,
> in every version is not gain but loss.

CHOSEN BROADSHEET POETS

Colin Bancroft, 31, is currently studying for an MA in Poetry at Manchester Metropolitan University under the tutelage of Jean Sprackland. He has previously had poems published in *Acumen*, *Broken Wine*, *Cannon's Mouth*, *The Copperfield Review*, *Elbow Room*, *LondonGrip* and *ScreechOwl*. He has also been shortlisted for both the Manchester Bridgewater Prize and the New Holland Press competition.

Missing mates

From Empson and Owen.

'Gas! Gas! Quick, boys! – An ecstasy of fumbling'

Slowly, the poison the whole blood stream fills;
Clambering over rusted wires,
The air remains, the air remains and kills.

Invading our systems, clear sight swills;
Clawing through mud filled mires,
Slowly, the poison the whole blood stream fills;

Cries commix, manic airborne shrills –
While slowly from life lungs retire;
The air remains, the air remains and kills.

From eyes and mouths thin dark blood spills
As crippled organs at last expire;
Slowly, the poison the whole blood stream fills;

They stop, life force slowly chills,
Shells turn homes into burning pyres.
The air remains, the air remains and kills.

It is the names you have lost, the ills
From missing mates, at which your heart conspires;
Slowly, the poison the whole blood stream fills;
The air remains, the air remains and kills.

Seven Days

A week. A week. Seven sleeps
You'd be free. Back to Blighty,
Across the waves – instead you're laid
Out in your grave – beneath
Your bone white, toothy slab.
In formation with sons, brothers, dads.
To think of all the things you'd done,
Dodged – hissing gas, wailing shells,
Passing bells, monstrous gun –
The blessings of the kind old sun.

A week. A week. Seven days;
On its way a telegram. Rehashed
Words that tell a mam her
Oldest boy is dead. For a sluice
Ditch in some foreign field.
People wheel, hoot and shout –
Armistice bells ringing out.
But in your house; behind those lines,
Your mother gasps, pulls down her blinds.

Remembrance Day

Bands march in time down the street
At the statue mourners meet,
Bugles sound and flags are raised
A duties hush enwraps the day.

The vicar reads a poignant psalm,
Veterans stand with hoisted arms
The people pray, 'Lest we forget'
Poppies placed upon the step.

While out on some Afghani road
A hidden IED explodes,
Another British soldier dies
For Freedom, Hope – a pack of lies.

Edwin Evans-Thirlwell is an editor and journalist at Future

Publishing in London, where he writes about videogames and digital culture. Aged 28, he has been published in *Brittle Star*, *Said and Done*, *The Guardian* and *The Mirror*. His present projects include a short fiction series about the dilemmas of eating, and a collection of poems about the Voyager 1 space probe.

The Great War (PC, PS4, Xbox One)

You may skip our intro: shovels biting
A refuge, the serried slog from depot
To dugout, the shapeless interludes spent
Filling the future's sack with consequence.
Don't stand for the camera as they stood
For gods and kings and countries – it's vital
To keep moving. Our trenches are roller
Coasters of authenticity – witness,
For instance, the artfulness of our rats,
The regional accents, the wizened tin,
The manpower expended on the wire.
Ours not to celebrate but execute
Their memory, boiled down to hands and eyes,
The aiming and surviving of a gun.

There were times, I admit, when we doubted.
The concept hasn't aged well. No Man's Land
Retains a timeless, turbulent appeal
But what of these 'tanks' – abortive oblongs
Shoved into the wire, whirring like stuck flies?
What of the over-powered artillery?
Ours, I'm sad to say, is the lesser War –
No offence meant to the injured parties
But you can't beat Dresden or Stalingrad,
Or the goose-step and kamikaze dive.

Liberties are taken at a decent
Remove. Existence dwindles to distance
As a bayonet shrinks to a stab wound,
Discohering over tumbled assets
Through thickets of low-res rubble to where
The horizon flattens into pictures.
Up ahead a slaughtered horse eye-catches,
Its grey guts achieving technicolours
While poppies bang like broken metaphors.
There's not enough silicon for the Somme.

Angela Kirby

On the Writing of War Poetry

'Can civilians write war poetry?' asked Adam O'Riordan. It's a fair question; one he answered by claiming that some of the finest poems on war in recent years have come from civilians, naming in particular Tony Harrison. But the right of a non-participant to speak in the voices of the victims of war, or of others who have seen active service, remains questionable, reminiscent of concerns raised in post war debates as to whether or not a gentile could or should write about the holocaust. We who experience war at second hand, as mere observers or as relatives of combatants, may find an oblique approach the only acceptable way to deal with the subject; only tangentially do we feel able or entitled to write about war's realities. Even Paul Celan, a survivor of the camps, struggled to write directly about what he had seen and undergone. In his most famous poem, 'Todesfugue' (Death Fugue), he wrote

> Black milk of daybreak we drink it at evening
> we drink it at midday and morning we drink it at night
> we drink and we drink
> we shovel a grave in the air there you won't lie too cramped

Born in 1932, twelve years after the end of the Great War and seven years before the outbreak of World War Two, I soon became aware of an unspoken sadness in my extended family, still mourning the death of my father's brother, killed during one of the last cavalry charges, in October 1918, aged twenty-one. Yet the war was seldom discussed and it is only recently that I have begun to write about it. Perhaps because of its centenary and the 70th anniversary of D Day, both wars have begun to obsess me.

In September, 1939, I was sitting under the kitchen table when Chamberlain announced that we were now at war with Germany, 'In and Out of the Kitchen' recalls this.

> In the kitchen, Hilda and Nancy
> are singing: Red sails in the sunset,
> they sing, red sails on the sea, but
> the silent child who is sitting there

beneath the long scrubbed table
floats out on the dog's red cushion
into a sky as red as the tomatoes
Hilda and Nancy are bottling, while
a man on the wireless says I have
to tell you that no such message has
been received, and Hilda and Nancy
stop singing, That's it, then, says Hilda,
and We'll be for it, says Nancy ....

I watched my four brothers join up; two were badly wounded, all were traumatized to a greater or lesser degree. My three sisters were also in the services, witnesses to death and suffering.

One of the first war poems I wrote was 'Early Mass, 1943'

Vere dignum et justum est ... it seems right to be
so hungry and so cold, offering Mass for those at war,
our stranger-fathers, our round-eyed brothers and sisters
gawky in caps and uniforms too large, too stiff for them ...

An elder sister made sure I was immersed in poetry, introducing me to works that most would have considered unsuitable for a five year old, including those of the war poets. Long before I could comprehend anything of the meaning, their words and rhythms became woven into me, but it was only when I began to write my own war poetry that I finally understood their tragic profundity.

'Foxholes', the first war poem of mine to be published, describes a brother's return from occupied France and his subsequent nightmares, how it seemed to me as a child.

Back from France by small boats
and night trains,
the last one stopping
to let him down in the wet fields ...

in at last to the kitchen,
where some mornings
we'd find him there asleep.
spark out on the dog-haired sofa ...

for years after there were times
when the dreams came back
till we grew used to it, waking
to shouts and screams,
to the glimpses of him
struggling naked in his damp
and foxy bed.

It was only through the memories and writings of others that I experienced
the First World War, only as a child and young teenager that I went through
the Second. Not until the death of a grandson in Afghanistan was I faced as
an adult with the terrible truth of conflict. It was two years before I could
write about this, and then only a short meditation on his funeral.

How It Is

i.m. Royal Marine Sam Alexander MC

Trestles slid away, folded
and put aside, candles snuffed
the singing stops, the music
dies, mourners drift off
and regroup by the gate.

Dear God, there seems
so little now to show for it all
nothing but a rolled-up flag
a scatter of wreaths, a bugle call
this shock of fresh-dug earth.

Later, the same experience fed into the poem 'Hellebores' in which a
woman gardens as she grieves for her son

leaves push up in spring,
the waiting gets harder.
At last the down-turned
flowers-heads come. One by
one, she turns their wan and

freckled faces upwards,
picks six stems, places them
in the silver vase she keeps
besides the photograph
and the framed medals.

A newer poem also concerns, in part, the death of that grandson who, like so many I have loved, died in May, a month which should be full of life and promise.

death is lilac, hawthorn, lilies of the valley, white roses,
death is larkrise, the thrush's song, the cuckoo's call …

Recently I saw a letter written in 1918 by a soldier servant to the wife of an officer in which he describes finding the missing officer's horse and the body of my uncle. Later, a friend told me of a letter he'd seen from a veteran who regularly visited the war graves in France. These are the roots of a poem about the Imperial War Museum. Then I found a black and white photograph of my six surviving uncles on holiday together in 1928, and was struck by the contrast between their seeming relaxation in the sun and the traces of strain on their faces. This led to the poem, 'On Anglesey'.

Certainly Rhosneigr, most probably August –
in my mother's hand, Picnic at the beach! 1928.
Ten years back from Gallipoli and the Somme,
six uncles lean against Lion Rock, captured
there by her Box Brownie, seemingly at ease, sun
warmed at the sea's edge, Gold Flakes in hand …

Four thousand years ago the Sumerian poet and priestess Enheduanna wrote of the destruction of temples, of blood in the streets., blood flowing down mountains. In 'It Could have Been Me', Clare Shaw wrote about an eight year old girl shot by US troops in Afkat in 2009. So little changes.

It could have been me on that street
with you in my hand
and my hands red and wet ...

Harry Guest

Patch Work

Poetry's written like a tapestry.
Each word's a stitch however tucked away
from text or happening as grey for cloud
or lazy green for foliage. All counts –
each article (in- or just definite)
must be considered (cut? left in? misplaced?).
The whole's a harmony, obscure perhaps
at first – what is that goddess doing? why
clauses to part the satrap from his verb? –
but not including what's irrelevant
(or forces hues and adjectives to clash)
and leaving nothing out which tells the tale
(or illustrates some gesture with a sword).
All language handed down is for our use
like tints on silk or wool, gold wire or glue.
Carpet of flowers may be a cliché but
can fill that lower right-hand corner where
the water's fringed with reeds like lashes round
a giant's eye. We keep all coinages –
a crescent moon, curved like a backwards C,
nail-paring, sickle moon – familiar,
available, a half-quotation, blurred,
unlocked by memory, decoded, penned –
no need to '*make it new*'. Inventions more
bizarre, more striking ('*easeful death*', '*enisled*',
'*outrageous fortune*', '*gong-tormented*') need
protection in quotation-marks to guard
such one-offs from pollution and contempt
till literacy itself is lost for ever.
Kind poets sometimes re-arrange a choice
of clips from old collections and that's fun
and friendly though could be a cheapening
of filched trouvailles – not that as time flows on
that matters. Soon attention-spans will last
three seconds at the most – a haiku will

prove far too taxing. Brecht contended that
bad poets borrow but good poets steal –
an easy joke to grin at, toss away.
The fabric sewn with care has worth outside
all rules seeking the unattainable
which Mallarmé identified once as
'the flower not there in all bouquets'. Somewhere –
nowhere we know nor ever can – there thrives
perfection, words beyond our reach, a scent
unrecognisable, a chord not heard,
blooms botanists can neither find nor name.

David Jones – Inscription lamenting the demise of Wales' heroes

250

Biographies

Timothy Adès, a rhyming translator-poet, has had over forty Brecht poems published. His books include Victor Hugo's *How to be a Grandfather*, and from Agenda Editions, Jean Cassou's *The Madness of Amadis*, and (in prospect) Robert Desnos's *Storysongs/Chantefables* with pictures by Cat Zaza: in bilingual text.

Donald Avery was, until 2010, librarian of a bioethics study centre in London, where he has lived since 1971. Elected a Member of the Royal Photographic Society in 1972, he is today a senior member of the British Titanic Society and of the website *Encyclopedia Titanica*. Born and educated in Canada, he first won the UNB Alumni Prize for Poetry at 16. Donald has written and recited his poetry since *Agenda* was founded, and is currently forming what will be a fifth collection.

Juliet Aykroyd won third prize in the Strokestown International Competition 2009, and was shortlisted in 2013. In 2012 she was shortlisted in the Wells and Torbay Poetry Competitions. Her poems have appeared in *The Interpreter's House*, *Vision* and *Indigo*. She is also a playwright, and won first prize in the Oz Whitehead/ IrishPen Competition for her play *Nancy Cunard*. She is currently working on a verse drama based on the life of the World War 2 poet Alun Lewis.

Mike Barlow has won a number of competitions, including the 2006 National Poetry Competition. His pamphlet *Amicable Numbers* (2008 Templar) was a Poetry Book Society Pamphlet Choice. His third full collection is *Charmed Lives* (Smith Doorstop 2012). website:www.mikebarlow.org.uk

Clare Best's poetry has been published since 2002 in a wide range of literary magazines including *Poetry News*, *The Rialto*, *Magma*, *The North*, *The London Magazine*, *Smiths Knoll*, *Agenda*, *Resurgence* and in many anthologies. Poems have been broadcast on BBC Radio 3 and on BBC Radio Lincolnshire. Clare's first full collection, *Excisions*, was shortlisted for the Seamus Heaney Centre Prize. She is working on a new collection of poems, and is collaborating with the painter Mary Anne Aytoun-Ellis on a project (supported by the South Downs National Park) that explores hidden and mysterious bodies of water across the South Country of England. Clare teaches Creative Writing for Brighton University and the Open University.

Alison Brackenbury was born in 1953. Her work has received an Eric Gregory and a Cholmondeley Award. Her eighth collection is *Then* (Carcanet, 2013). New poems can be read at her website: www.alisonbrackenbury.co.uk

Peter Carpenter was born in Ewell in 1957; he is a poet, essayist and teacher; he co-edits Worple Press www.worplepress.co.uk. *Just Like That* (Smith Doorstop, 2012), a 'New and Selected Poems', followed five previous collections. He wrote a chapter on the roles of creative writing for the *OUP Handbook of Contemporary British and Irish Poetry* (OUP 2012) and is a contributor to Iain Sinclair's *London: City of Disappearances*.

Martin Caseley is an English teacher, essayist and poet, living in Stamford, Lincolnshire. He regularly contributes reviews to *Stride* magazine website (www.stridemagazine.co.uk) and his most recent poetry collection, *A Sunday Map of The World*, appeared in 2000. He is working on new poems and essays.

Robert Chandler studied Russian at Leeds University and spent the academic year 1973-74 as a British Council exchange scholar in Voronezh, a large city 200 miles south of Moscow. His translations of Sappho and Apollinaire are published in the series 'Everyman's Poetry', but he is best known for his translations from Russian. These include Alexander Pushkin's *The Captain's Daughter*, Vasily Grossman's *Everything Flows*, *The Road* and *Life and Fate*, many works by Andrey Platonov and Hamid Ismailov's novel *The Railway*, set in Central Asia. He has compiled two anthologies for Penguin Classics, of Russian short stories and Russian magic tales. A third anthology, *The Penguin Book of Russian Poetry*, will be published in February 2015. He is also the author of a B*rief Life* of Alexander Pushkin. For the last seven years he has taught classes in literature and in translation, part-time, at Queen Mary College, University of London. He also works as a mentor for the BCLT mentorship scheme. His translations have won prizes in both the UK and the USA and his co-translation of Vasily Grossman's *An Armenian Sketchbook* is currently shortlisted for the PEN Translation Prize.

Stephen Claughton read English at Oxford and worked for 34 years as a civil servant in London. His poems have appeared in *The Interpreter's House*, *Iota*, *London Grip*, *Other Poetry* and *The Warwick Review* and have been accepted by *Poetry Salzburg Review*. He has twice been nominated for the Forward Best Single Poem Prize.

D. V. Cooke (David Vincent Cooke) was born in Cheshire and graduated in English from London University. He worked for a number of years for The Poetry Library in London and has published in numerous poetry magazines including: *Acumen, Babel, Envoi, Frogmore Papers, Orbis, Outposts, Poetry Wales, Stand, Swansea Review, Tandem* and *Agenda*.

Belinda Cooke was born in Reading in 1957. She completed her PhD on Robert Lowell's interest in Osip Mandelstam in 1993. She has published three books to date: *Resting Place* (Flarestack Publishing, 2008); *Paths of the Beggarwoman: Selected Poems of Marina Tsvetaeva*, (Worple Press, 2008) and (with Richard McKane) *Flags* by Boris Poplavsky, (Shearsman Press, 2009). She and Richard are currently working on Boris Pasternak's later poems and her latest collection *Stem* is forthcoming.

David Cooke's retrospective collection, *In the Distance*, was published in 2011 by Night Publishing. A new collection, *Work Horses*, was published by Ward Wood in 2012. HIs poems and reviews have appeared in journals such as *Agenda, The Bow Wow Shop, The Irish Press, The London Magazine, Magma, The North, Poetry Ireland Review, Poetry London, Poetry Salzburg Review, The Reader, The SHOp, Stand* and *The Use of English*. A new collection to be called *A Murmuration* is scheduled for publication by Two Rivers Press in 2015.

Clare Crossman has published two collections of poetry with Shoestring Press, *The Shape of Us 2010 and Vanishing Point 2013*. Her poems have been included in *A Room to Live In,* A Kettle's Yard Anthology, and Contourlines New Responses to Landscape *In Word and Image*. She lives outside Cambridge.

Martyn Crucefix's most recent full collection, *Hurt*, was published by Enitharmon. His translation of Rainer Maria Rilke's *Duino Elegies* (Enitharmon 2006) was shortlisted for the 2007 Popescu Prize for European Poetry Translation. His translation of Rilke's *Sonnets to Orpheus* (Enitharmon) was published in 2012. *The Time We Turned* (Shearsman, 2014) and *A Hatfield* Mass (Worple Press, 2014) have both recently appeared. For blog and more visit http://www.martyncrucefix.com

Michael Curtis grew up in Liverpool, attended Oxford and Sheffield universities, worked in library and cultural services and lives in Kent. He is widely published in magazines and anthologies and has given readings and workshops in England, Ireland, the Isle of Man, Belgium, France, Finland, Germany, Latvia and Cyprus. His work has been broadcast on radio in England, Ireland, Romania and Latvia. *Horizon*, a collection of poems set on the Isle of Man, was launched at the first Manx Litfest in 2012 and his latest collection, *The Fire in Me Now*, was published by Cultured Llama in autumn 2014.

Tony Curtis was born in Dublin in 1955. He studied literature at Essex University and Trinity College Dublin. An award-winning poet, Curtis has published nine warmly received collections. He is well known in Ireland for his work in primary schools, prisons, asylums. His most recent collections are: *Pony* (Occasional Press 2013) with the painter Dave Liburn; *Folk* (Arc Publications 2011); *An Elephant Called Rex and a Dog Called Dumbo – an A to Z of poems for children*, with illustrations by Pat Mooney, 2011. Last year also saw the publication of *Island Currach* (Real Ireland 2012), a haiku and tanka book with photographs by Liam Blake. Curtis has been awarded the Irish National Poetry Prize and the Varuna House Exchange Fellowship to Australia. He is a member of Aosdana.

Terry Dammery was born in Hexham, spent his early years in London orphanages and subsequently worked as an Aircraft Engineer, a Head of English in a UK comprehensive school and a University Lecturer in the UK and Singapore. He now lives in the English Peak District with his family and is one half of the Edale Poets. His contribution is from 'Chasing Butterflies' – poems about collateral damage.

Hilary Davies has published three collections of poetry from Enitharmon: *The Shanghai Owner of the Bonsai Shop; In a Valley of This Restless Mind*, which includes poem sequences about the love affair between the 12th century philosopher, Peter Abelard, and his gifted pupil, Héloïse; and *Imperium*, containing an evocation of the naval conflict of the Napoleonic Wars. Hilary won an Eric Gregory award in 1983, has been a Hawthornden Fellow, Chairman of the Poetry Society, and 1st prizewinner in the Cheltenham Literature Festival poetry competition. She was Head of Languages at St. Paul's Girls' School for 19 years and is currently Royal Literary Fund Fellow at King's College, London. Hilary was married to the poet and editor, Sebastian Barker, who died in January 2014.

John F. Deane was born on Achill Island 1943; founded *Poetry Ireland* and *The Poetry Ireland Review*, 1979; published several collections of poetry and some fiction; Won the *O'Shaughnessy Award for Irish Poetry*, the *Marten Toonder Award* for Literature, *Golden Key award* from Serbia, *Laudomia Bonanni Prize* from L'Aquila, Italy. Shortlisted for both the T.S.Eliot prize and The Irish Times Poetry Now Award, won residencies in Bavaria, Monaco and Paris. He is a member of Aosdána . His recent poetry collections: *Eye of the Hare*, came from Carcanet 2011. *Snow falling on Chestnut Hill: New & Selected Poems* was published by Carcanet in October 2012. His latest fiction is a novel, *Where No Storms Come, published* by Blackstaff in 2010. He is current editor of *Poetry Ireland Review*.

Tom Dilworth teaches at the University of Windsor, in Ontario, is the author of over a hundred articles on Romantic poetry and modern literature. His recent books include: David Jones's *Wedding Poems*, The *Rime of the Ancient Mariner* illustrated by David Jones, *David Jones in The Great War*, and a book of poetry entitled *Here Away*. He has written *David Jones, Engraver, Soldier, Painter, Poet*, a biography to be published by Jonathan Cape.

Mac Donald Dixon is a Caribbean Writer, born on the island of Saint Lucia. His work has appeared in several literary magazines, including *Caribbean Quarterly, Bim, Calalloo, Caribbean Writer, Wasafari* and *Agenda*. In addition to poetry, Dixon has written several plays, published three novels and a collection of short stories. In 1994 he received the Saint Lucia Medal of Merit for his contribution to Literature and photography. In 2006 he was honoured by Saint Lucia's Cultural development Foundation with a lifetime achievement award.

Mary Durkin, 62, is retired, formerly in local government. She has published previously in *Magma, Acumen*, and *The SHOp*, and has two further poems accepted for publication this year. She lives in central London.

Gerrit Engelke (German, 1890-1918) was born to poor parents and apprenticed to a house-painter. His poetry upholds spiritual values against industrialisation and war. He died of wounds, just before the Armistice. *Die Zeit* in 1956 called him a forgotten German poet.

Edmund Gray was involved with *Agenda* from the beginning, and was a trustee for decades; He was born in 1939; educated at Westminster and Magdalen College, Oxford; worked in publishing, higher education and as an Inspector of Historic Buildings; fenced for Wales for several years; now works as a writer in Oxford; has written a history of the British house and five other books.

Richard Greene is a Canadian poet and biographer. His third collection of poems, *Boxing the Compass*, won Canada's most prestigious prize, The Governor General's Literary Award, in 2010. He has recently published a new collection *Dante's House*. He is the editor of the letters of Graham Greene and author of a controversial biography of Edith Sitwell. He is a professor at the University of Toronto, where he serves as director of the MA in Creative Writing.

John Greening received a Cholmondeley award in 2008. His latest collections are *To the War Poets* (Carcanet), *Knot* (Worple) and *Poetry Masterclass* (Greenwich Exchange). His edition of Edmund Blunden appears from OUP in Spring 2015. He is currently collaborating with Penelope Shuttle on a book about Hounslow Heath.

Edward Greenwood was born in 1933. He studied English Literature at Oxford from 1951 to 1956 and then taught it at the University of Kent from 1966 to 1992. He is now an Honorary Research Fellow in English Literature at the University of Kent. He has had articles in many journals including *Essays In Criticism, Twentieth Century, The Listener* and *Encounter*. In 1975 he published *The Comprehensive Vision*, a study of Tolstoy. He brought out a British Council pamphlet on F. R. Leavis in 1978. He has written poetry since boyhood and has published privately several pamphlets of poetry.

Stuart Henson's books include *The Impossible Jigsaw* and *Ember Music* from Peterloo Poets and *A Place Apart* (Shoestring Press). His most recent collection is *The Odin Stone* (Shoestring, 2011).

Recently The Poetry Archive recorded poems by **Harry Guest** from the 1950s onwards and several of his poems have this year been deftly translated by Anne Mounic (poet, novelist and literary academic at the Sorbonne) in the magazine *Peut-Être* and its sibling on line *Temporel*.

Chris Hardy's poems have been published widely in magazines, including *Agenda, Poetry Review*, the *Rialto* and the *North*, and in anthologies and websites. He has won prizes in the National Poetry Society's, and other, competitions. His third collection, *Write Me a Few Of Your Lines,* was published by Graft Poetry in 2012. Chris is in LiTTLe MACHiNe (little-machine.com). "The most brilliant music and poetry band in the world". Carol Ann Duffy.

Geoffrey Heptonstall is a poetry reviewer for *The London Magazine*. He writes regular commentaries on politics and culture for *Open Democracy*. He is a widely-published poet, essayist and reviewer. His recent performance work includes scripts for Kilter Theatre, Newton's Heritage and White Rabbit companies, and the festivals at Bolton, Canterbury, Dunbar and the Wirral.

Ian Higgins has published critical anthologies of First and Second World War French poetry for student use. Among his translations are Pierre Seghers's long poem *Piranesi* (Forest Books); prose and verse by nine French writers in *The Lost Voices of World War I*, ed. Tim Cross (Bloomsbury); *Florilegium*, texts by Francis Ponge with engravings by Jane Kennelly (Epsilon); French poems in *We Are the Dead – Poems and Paintings of the Great War, 1914–1918*, ed. David Roberts (Red Horse) and in *The Hundred Years' War*, ed. Neil Astley (Bloodaxe); and most recently, Albert-Paul Granier's wonderful Great War poems, *Cockerels and Vultures* (Saxon Books). He is currently translating some twenty poets with a view to a full anthology of Great War French poetry in English, to be published by Saxon Books in 2016.

Matthew Howard is 35 years old and has had poems in several magazines including *The Reader*, *Poetry Salzburg Review* and *Stand*, with poems in the current issues of *The North* and *The Rialto*. Matt was chosen as one of The Poetry Trust's *Masterclass* participants for this year's Aldeburgh Poetry Festival. Matt lives in Norwich where he works full time for the RSPB as a fundraiser.

Karen Izod is a consultant, academic and writer working independently in the field of organisational and cultural change, and is the author of a number of academic articles and books. Karen has recently published poetry and creative non-fiction in the *Journal of Attachment Studies*, and focuses on attachment to landscape and memories that weave through generations.

Roland John has had a long association with *Agenda*. Agenda Editions published his first full collection *Believing Words are Real* in 1985. His prose books include A *Beginner's Guide to The Cantos of Ezra Pound*. His latest poetry collection is *A Lament for England*. He is currently working on a new collection and his *Selected Poems*.

Anna Johnson was recently awarded her DPhil, entitled 'Art and artefact in the writings of David Jones' from Brasenose College, Oxford. She is interested in the link between Jones's poetry and visual art, and her thesis places his art theories and practice within the broader context of the visual cultures of British Modernism. She is now based at St Anne's College, Oxford. She has published a chapter on David Jones's use of Old English, 'Wounded men and wounded trees: David Jones and the Anglo-Saxon Culture Tangle', in *Anglo-Saxon Culture and the Modern Imagination*, eds. Dr Nicholas Perkins & Dr David Clark (Boydell & Brewer, 2010). In September 2014 she co-convened a conference 'David Jones: Christian Modernist?' at St Anne's College and Regent's Park College, Oxford.

Peter Kahn is a founding member of the London poetry collective, Malika's Kitchen. As a Visiting Fellow at Goldsmiths, he was the founder of the Spoken Word Education Training Programme. His poems have been published internationally, including in the *Bellingham Review, Jelly Bucket, The Roanoke Review, Lumina, Make* and *The Fourth River*. He is a commended poet in the Poetry Society's National Poetry Competition (UK) and was a finalist in the Fugue Poetry Contest, among other competitions and the co-editor of the Golden Shovel Anthology honouring Gwendolyn Brooks. A high school teacher since 1994, Peter was a Featured Speaker at the National Council for the Teachers of English annual convention.

David Kerridge was born near London in 1943. He worked for the BMA in London for six years then moved to Paris in 1970, where he has been a teacher, and translator of medical documents. During the 70s, he had a number of poems and short stories published, and in the last twenty years has written text books and articles for UK and French publishers. Recently, he has had prose accepted for publication in *The French Literary Review* and poems in *Agenda*. David very sadly died just before this journal went to print.

Frances-Anne King's work has appeared in many prize winning anthologies and journals, including *Acumen, Agenda, Envoi, The British Journal of Psychiatry, The Rialto, New Walk, Poetry Ireland Review, Poetry Salzburg Review* and *Poetry Wales*. Her first pamphlet, *Weight of Water*, was published by Poetry Salzburg in 2013. In 2012 she started the *Ekphrastic Poetry Workshop Series* at the Holburne Museum in Bath.

Angela Kirby's poems are widely published in journals, have won prizes and commendations in several major competitions and have been read on BBC TV and Radio Four. Much of her work is translated into Romanian. Her collections from Shoestring Press are *Mr. Irresistible*, 2005, *Dirty Work*, 2008, *A Scent of Winter*, 2013. A fourth collection is underway.

David Kuhrt was born in 1940. After a year spent in Germany, following ten years teaching art and running a youth centre with ILEA, he went to Martinique where he illustrated *Contes Créoles de la Martinique*, then returned to start a sign-making business, using glass and inverse-relief gilded letters. Imitating a method used on French turn-of the-last-century Parisian signs, he and his then partner/wife provided some 200 such signs for J D Wetherspoon from 1982-2000. He is currently collating poetry going back to the 60s and looking for a publisher.

Laozi (also Lao-Tzu or Lao-tze) was a philosopher and poet of ancient China. A legendary figure, usually dated to around the 6th century BCE, he is reckoned a contemporary of Confucius. The reputed author of the *Daodejing* (or *Tao Te Ching*), founder of philosophical Daoism.

Gill Learner lives in Reading. Her poems have been widely published in journals such as *Acumen, Mslexia, Poetry News* and *Smiths Knoll*, and a variety of anthologies. It has also won a number of awards including the Poetry Society's Hamish Canham Prize 2008 and the English Association's Fellows' Poetry

Prize 2012. Her first collection, *The Agister's Experiment*, was published by Two Rivers Press in 2011. She reads regularly at Reading's Poets' Café.

Karen Leeder is Professor of Modern German Literature and Fellow and Tutor in German at New College, Oxford. She has published widely on modern German literature, especially poetry, and is also a prize-winning translator of German poetry into English.

Jane Lovell lives in Warwickshire where she is Head of Early Years at a Midlands Prep School. She runs the Warwickshire Poetry Stanza for the Poetry Society and her poems have appeared in a range of publications including *Poetry Wales, Myslexia, Envoi* and webzine *Ink, Sweat & Tears*.

Sue Mackrell teaches Creative Writing at Loughborough University. Her poems and short stories have been published in anthologies and magazines and in a poetry collection, *Rhythms*. She is co-director of Crystal Clear Creators, a not-for-profit organisation committed to promoting new writing. She is currently working on a Heritage Lottery funded project exploring the experiences of those on the Home Front in Leicester during the First World War.

Char March is an award-winning poet and playwright for stage and BBC Radio 4. Her latest collections are *The Cloud Appreciation Society's Day Out* and *The Thousand Natural Shocks* (pub. Indigo Dreams). She has been a Hawthornden Fellow twice, and has just completed her contract as Writer-in-Residence for the NHS in North West England. Born in West Hartlepool County Durham, **Martin Malone** now lives in Warwickshire. A winner of the 2011 Straid Poetry Award and the 2012 Mirehouse Prize , his first full collection, *The Waiting Hillside*, is published by Templar Poetry. Currently studying for a Ph.D in poetry at Sheffield University, he edits *The Interpreter's House* poetry journal.

Stuart Medland has written two collections of poems for children, composed whilst still a primary school teacher in Norfolk. Much of his writing is inspired by natural history and his *Rings in the Shingle*, published by Brambleby Books, is a poetic celebration of Norfolk wildlife inspired by his own photographic encounters. *Ouzel on the Honister*, a volume of poems distilled from his many visits to the Lake District over the years, is currently in preparation. Stuart is a regular contributor to *Agenda* and a collection of poems about his father, *Last Man Standing*, is now available from *Agenda Editions*.

Merryn McCarthy now lives in the Gers region of South West France. For many years she was Head of English in various schools. Her poems have been published in many magazines and journals in Ireland and the UK, and her collection, *Playing Truant*, was published by Agenda Editions.

Michael Mc Carthy is a West Cork born poet living in North Yorkshire. A winner of the Patrick Kavanagh Award, his most recent collection *At the Races* was the overall winner of the Poetry Business Competition judged by Michael Longley. A new collection, *The Healing Station*, is due out from The Poetry Business in 2015.

Jennifer A. McGowan obtained her MA and PhD from the University of Wales and, despite being certified as disabled at age 16, has persevered and has published poetry and prose in many magazines and anthologies on both sides of the Atlantic. She has been Highly Commended in the Torbay Poetry Competition. Her chapbooks are available from Finishing Line Press. Her website, with more poetry and examples of her mediaeval calligraphy, can be found at http://www.jenniferamcgowan.com . Handwritten and calligraphed copies of some of her published poems can be purchased from http://www. handwrittenpoems.co.uk/product-category/poems/jennifer-mcgowan/

Christine McNeill has published four poetry collections, the latest *First and Last Music* (Shoestring Press, 2014). She has contributed widely to literary journals and magazines.

David Mohan is based in Dublin, Ireland, and received a PhD in English literature from Trinity College. He has been published in or has work forthcoming in *Stand, Acumen, Envoi, Poetry Salzburg Review, Popshot, Structo, Orbis* and *KaffeeKlatsch*. In 2012 he won the Café Writers' International Poetry Competition. His poetry has been shortlisted for The Bridport Prize.

Eric Morgan was brought up in Gower, did National Service, then gained a degree in geography and teacher training in the University of Aberystwyth. World War 2 was just over when he was called up to the post-war army as a sergeant in the Education Corps. He spent the rest of his life teaching in a grammar school in Gwent/Monmouthshire, then in a Teacher Training College at Newcastle, and the Polytechnic. He lived there for 47 years. Now retired, he lives in Oxford.

Tim Murdoch lives partly in Spain and partly in Surrey. He is a healer, and has appeared over the years in *Agenda*, and elsewhere. His new poetry collection is forthcoming.

Ruth O'Callaghan has been translated into six languages and has read extensively in Asia, Europe and the USA – where she also completed a successful successful TV/Reading tour in New York and Boston.

She is a competition adjudicator, interviewer, reviewer, editor, workshop leader and mentor. Her sixth collection *An Unfinished Sufficiency* is due to be published in 2015.

Richard Ormrod is a published biographer, journalist and reviewer. He is currentlywriting the authorised biography of the poet Andrew Young and is working towards his own first volume of poems. He is married and lives in East Sussex and was, for some years, a Head of English in several schools in Kent.

Mario Petrucci is a multi-award-winning poet and residency frontiersman, the only poet to have held residencies at the Imperial War Museum and with BBC Radio 3. Petrucci aspires to "Poetry on a geological scale" (*Verse*). *i tulips* (Enitharmon, 2010) takes its name from Petrucci's vast Anglo-American sequence, whose "modernist marvels" (*Poetry Book Society*) convey his distinctive combination of innovation and humanity. www.mariopetrucci.com

Olive M. Ritch has been published in a number of literary journals and anthologies including *Causeway/Cabhsair*, The *Hippocrates Prize 2011* and *Don't Bring Me No Rocking Chair*. She received a commendation in the National Poetry Competition 2003 and won the Calder Prize for Poetry at the University of Aberdeen in 2006.

James Roberts lives in Hay-on-Wye. Recent poetry has appeared in *Agenda* and *Envoi*, essays in *Earthlines* and *The Island Review*.

Robert Smith is a Londoner who now lives in Cambridge. His poetry is strongly influenced by music, and makes vivid use of imagery for its effects. He has been published previously in *Agenda*.

Ruth Smith used to teach English but now spends her time travelling and writing poems. Poems have been published most recently in *The South Bank Magazine* and *Obsessed with Pipework* with two upcoming in *The New Walk Magazine*. Work has appeared in many anthologies including *Entering The Tapestry* produced by The Poetry School.

S.K. Smith lives in Canterbury.

Gerard Smyth was born in Dublin where he still lives. His seventh collection, *The Fullness of Time: New and Selected Poems* (Dedalus Press, Dublin) was published in 2010 and appeared in an Italian translation last year. He was the 2012 recipient of the O'Shaughnessy Poetry Award from the University of St Thomas in Minnesota. He is co-editor of *If Ever You Go: A Map of Dublin in Poetry and Song* (Dedalus) which was Dublin's One City One Book this year. He is a member of Aosdána and Poetry Editor of *The Irish Times*.

Robert Spencer was born in Peckham, London. After a career in the City and ten years running his own consultancy business he now farms sheep in Hadlow Down, East Sussex. He is a poet, playwright and artist and has just launched High Weald Poets as an offshoot of the Kent and Sussex Poetry Society. He has three recorded collections and a fourth is under way.

Robert Stein's first collection *The Very End of Air* came out in 2011. His poems have appeared in *Agenda* over the years a well as in *Poetry Review, Ambit, The Rialto, Envoi, The Wolf, Staple, Magma, Orbis* and elsewhere. 'Hommage De M. Erik Satie À Soi-Même' was commended in the 2012 National Poetry Competition.

N S Thompson has most recently co-edited with Andy Croft, *A Modern Don Juan: Cantos for These Times by Divers Hands* (Five Leaves, 2014). His *Letter to Auden* was published by Smokestack in 2010 and his work appears in *Agenda, Able Muse* (USA), *New Walk, The Spectator* and *Stand*. He is currently translating a major Italian crime trilogy for Quercus Editions and his translations of Italian poetry have appeared in *The Penguin Montale* and *The Faber Book of 20th-Century Italian Poems*.

Harriet Torr has had poems commended in the Arvon 2001 competition and the National competition 2008. Her pamphlet *My father's pot* was published by Koo poetry press in 2009.

Émile Verhaeren (1855-1916), a Fleming, is rated the leading Belgian poet to have written in French. For his vigour, great range, and breadth of vision, he has been compared to Victor Hugo and Walt Whitman. A volume has now appeared from Arc with Will Stone's translations into English.

Olivia Walwyn was born in 1983 and grew up in Norfolk. She studied English Literature and Philosophy at Durham University before going on to York University to do an MA in Political Philosophy. She now lives with her husband in Macclesfield and works as a school librarian. She has had poems published in *The Rialto, The North* and *Ariadne's Thread*.